THREE INVISIBLE MONSTERS

Who they are and how to fight them

THREE INVISIBLE MONSTERS

IRENE MELLACE

PROLOGUE

"Loved, always loved; respect yourself. Always take the time to pamper yourself, take care of yourself, make yourself beautiful, in the span of twenty-four hours never forget to cut out at least an hour to look in the mirror and ask yourself: am I really happy? Am I giving the best of myself by highlighting my best qualities in order to achieve it? Do I need help, advice, suggestions or material and emotional support to achieve my goal? But most of all, I set myself a good goal that gives my life meaning and makes it so worth living? I am surrounded by people who love me, appreciate me, understand me and help me in difficult moments? The contexts and situations that I live and surround me make me feel alive, thriving, productive or make me "fade", feel sad, dull and not valued? Can I discern good from evil, true from falsehood, right from wrong, positive from negative, reality from fiction, loyalty from deception and so on for a myriad of other expressions? From the answers you take, will you understand if the life you live is suitable for your standards, your dreams, your expectations or simply you

are repressing a strong sense of dissatisfaction that I repress adapting to a contest that does not really belong to me? In the long term, these situations will cause strange and ruthless physical situations that cause thousands and thousands of suicides every year around the world. In the next chapters we will see better together what this is all about, but in the meantime, let's not forget every day to ask ourselves these questions and write down on a piece of paper what satisfies us and what we would like to change radically."

Chapter I Who is anxiety?

At least once in our lives we have all heard of anxiety; but what, or rather, who is this monster? Anxiety is a term widely used to indicate a complex of cognitive, behavioural and physiological reactions that occur as a result of the perception of a stimulus considered threatening and against which we do not consider ourselves sufficiently capable to react. Anxiety itself, however, is not an abnormal phenomenon. It is a basic emotion, which involves a state of activation of the organism when a situation is perceived subjectively as dangerous.

Cognitive symptoms typical of anxiety are:

• the sense of mental emptiness;

• a growing sense of alarm and danger;

• induction of negative images, memories and thoughts;

• the implementation of protective cognitive behaviours;

• the marked feeling of being observed and being at the center of the attention of others.

In the human species anxiety translates into an immediate tendency to the exploration of the environment, in the search for explanations, reassurances and escape routes. The main instinctive anxiety management strategy is also the avoidance of the dreaded situation ("better safe than sorry" strategy - "better prevention than cure"). Protective and submission behaviors are also frequent (to be accompanied, to take anxiolytics to the need, etc.).

Anxiety is also often accompanied by physical and physiological manifestations such as:

• tension and tension

• tremor

• sweat

• palpitation

• increase in heart rate

• dizziness

• nausea

* *tingling at the ends and around the mouth*

* *derealization and depersonalization*

Below we will better describe some physical symptoms of anxiety, how they manifest and what are the possible consequences:

Palpitations,

As far as possible, it is necessary to distinguish different conditions related to palpitations: the heart, tachycardia and arrhythmia. The latter, for example, often occurs with irregular heartbeats even in healthy people, during their daily activities and is more likely to occur when the person is anxious. It can be induced by a number of agents such as nicotine, caffeine, alcohol and electrolyte imbalance. Often the interpretation given to such a physical symptom during an anxious state is linked to the idea of having a heart attack. This although at the base there is an increased electrophysiological excitability of the heart muscle which has no negative consequences from a medical point of view.

Chest pain

It is a physical symptom that can occur during periods of high anxiety in the absence of a heart disorder. It can therefore derive from different sources such as thoracic respiration and gastrointestinal disorders (e.g. esophageal reflux or esophageal spasms). When the person interprets catastrophically the benign causes of pain it is possible that the anxious state increases leading also to panic. But we actually know that when a very high state of anxiety emerges, the body secretes adrenaline that causes an increase in the heart rate and the body works faster. It is an evolutionary way to better prepare the person to manage dangerous situations. If adrenaline damaged the heart, how could man survive to this day? So, the acceleration of the heartbeat.

Feeling of shortness of breath

Breathing is an action that works regardless of what a person thinks or does, it is automatically controlled by the brain. In fact, brain controls also work when trying to stop breathing. The feeling of shortness of breath is very frequent in anxiety disorders and comes from prolonged and repeated chest respiration (pectoral). In fact, a physical response to stress is the relative dominance of chest respiration over the abdominal one, which leads to fatigue of intercostal muscles, straining and having spasms that cause discomfort and pectoral pains causing shortness of breath sensation. If you can't understand that these feelings are induced by chest breathing, then they will seem sudden.

Nausea or abdominal disorders

The stomach contracts and relaxes in a regular and constant way. When this rhythm is disturbed nausea occurs. Several factors can lead to this physical sensation such as ingestion of certain foods, vestibular disorders, postural hypotension or even previously neutral stimuli. The function of diet and digestion are the first to freeze during a state of alert, but if the person mistakenly interprets nausea as a sign of impending vomiting it is more likely that anxiety increases and leads to panic. But, fortunately, that nausea leads to vomiting rarely happens, it is more likely that people overestimate this possibility.

Tremors and Sweating

The first are involuntary movements, oscillators and rhythms of one or more parts of the body, caused by the alternating contraction of opposing muscle movements. Sweating instead helps to control body temperatures, which rises when you have been anxious. In fact, stress stimulates the sympathetic nervous system with increased levels of adrenaline and norepinephrine that stimulate an increase in metabolism, thus increasing the production of heat and the consequent sweating useful to the lowering of the body temperature. Again, the greater the *attention and the catastrophization with respect to such physical symptoms the greater the probability that these increase of intensity.*

Dizziness,

Vertigo is the product of the illusion of movement of self or the environment. They consist of feelings of confusion or dizziness, dizziness or stunning. When information from the balance system (visual, somatosensory and vestibular system) comes into conflict, vertigo occurs. Balance problems and associated physical symptoms (instability, anxiety, cold sweat, palpitations) can also occur as a result of anxiety, hyperventilation and stress-related reactions such as clenching the jaw and teeth. Obviously, the intensity of vertigo can increase if more attention is given to these feelings.

Derealisation or depersonalisation

Depersonalization (feeling of unreality) or depersonalization (feeling detached from oneself), are experiences that can be induced by tiredness, sleep deprivation, meditation, relaxation or the use of substances, alcohol and benzodiazepines. There are also other more subtle causes linked to short periods of sensory deprivation or reduction of sensory inputs, such as fixing a point on a wall for 3 minutes. The curious thing is that, even here, the vicious circle is established based on the interpretation given to these physical symptoms. When you experience depersonalization or derealization (experience that a third of the population has experienced) the more a person gets scared, the more he breathes, the more he gets oxygen (eliminating carbon dioxide) the more it increases the feeling of depersonalization or derealization.

Fear of Fear

The physical symptoms of anxiety often scare off by generating vicious circles, the so-called "fear of fear". However, they depend on the fact that, assuming that they are in a situation of real danger, the organism in anxiety needs the maximum muscular energy available, in order to escape or attack as effectively as possible, avoiding danger and ensuring survival. Anxiety, therefore, is not only a limit or a disorder, but is an important resource. It is in fact a physiological condition effective in many moments of life to protect us from risks, maintain the state of alert and improve performance (for example, when you are under examination). When the activation of the anxiety system is excessive, unjustified or disproportionate compared to situations, however, we are faced with an anxiety disorder, which can greatly complicate a person's life and make him unable to deal with even the most common situations.

The known and clearly diagnosable anxiety disorders are the following:

1- specific phobias

When we talk about phobias we usually refer to: dog phobia, cat phobia, spider phobia, phobia of enclosed spaces, phobia of insects, phobia of aircraft, phobia of blood, phobia of injections, etc. More precisely, there are generalized phobias (agoraphobia and social phobia), strongly disabling, and the common specific phobias, generally well managed by the subjects avoiding the feared stimuli, which are classified as follows: Animal type. Phobia of spiders (arachnophobia), phobia of birds or phobia of pigeons (ornithophobia), phobia of insects, phobia of dogs (cynophobia), phobia of cats (ailurophobia), phobia of mice, etc... Natural environment type. Phobia of thunderstorms (brontophobia), phobia of heights (acrophobia), phobia of darkness (scotofhobia), phobia of water (hydrophobia), etc... Blood-injection-wound type. Blood phobia (hemophobia), phobia of needles, phobia of syringes, etc... In general, if the fear is caused by the sight of blood or an injury or by receiving an injection or other invasive medical procedures. Situational type. In cases where fear is caused by a specific situation, such as public transport, tunnels, bridges, elevators, flying (aviophobia), driving, or enclosed places (claustrophobia or agoraphobia). In case the fear is triggered by other stimuli such as fear or avoidance of situations that could lead to suffocation or contracting of a disease (see also obsessive-compulsive disorder and hypochondria), etc. A particular form of phobia concerns one's own body or a part of it, which the person sees as hideous, unappealing, repugnant (dysmorphophobia). It is important to clarify that the type of phobia from which one is affected has no unconscious symbolic meaning, as suggested by some psychoanalysts, and the specific fear is linked solely to experiences of involuntary incorrect learning (not necessarily remembered by the subject), so the organism unintentionally associates danger to an object or situation objectively not dangerous. It is, in essence, a process of so-called "classical conditioning". This conditioning remains unchanged over time because of the spontaneous systematic avoidance that the phobic subjects put in place compared to the dreaded situation.

2- Agoraphobia

The term agoraphobia comes from the Greek word Agora which means square; in fact, the first uses of the word in psychology and psychiatry addressed people who were afraid to go to crowded places. In fact, patients with agoraphobia symptoms fear situations where it is difficult to escape or receive relief; as a result, they avoid such places in order to control the anxiety related to the prefiguration of a new panic crisis. In fact, in most cases, agoraphobia is a problem that emerges secondary to the onset of panic attacks or less anxiety crises; it occurs when the agoraphobic subject begins to systematically avoid all places, the situations and contexts in which there might be obstacles to the possibility of *being helped. Among the situations that are most frequently avoided by those showing symptoms of agoraphobia are: go out alone or stay home alone; drive or travel by car; wait crowded places such as markets or concerts; take the bus or airplane; be on a bridge or in an elevator. When these avoidances begin to compromise the daily activities and the socio-occupational functioning of the person then we speak of agoraphobia. Sometimes, the problem is more difficult to identify because the subject does not avoid certain feared situations but becomes unable to face them without the assistance of a trusted person. Agoraphobia can be diagnosed within the panic disorder with agoraphobia or as agoraphobia without history of panic disorder. In the latter case, the seizures that the patient avoids are characterized by panic-like anxiety symptoms, but without all the characteristics of the actual panic attack. Agoraphobia is characterized by symptoms such as: Anxiety linked to being in places where it would be difficult to get away, escape or ask for and receive help, in the event of a panic attack or an anxiety crisis. Feared situations are avoided or addressed with great difficulty or through the support of an escort. Anxiety and avoidance limit the socio-occupational functioning of the subject and do not arise from other types of fear or phobias (Avoid elevators for a claustrophobic, avoid social situations for the social phobic, avoid stimuli that recall a traumatic event in post-traumatic disorder stress). Within cognitive-behavioral psychotherapy, exposure techniques have proven useful in reducing behaviors that feed agoraphobic anxiety. Recently strategies have been implemented to increase the ability of the subjects to stay in contact with the anxious activation without fear of the catastrophic consequences, favoring acceptance and decreasing the need for control of anxiety symptoms. In general, however, psychotherapy is essential for the treatment of agoraphobia, while psychomedications, containing anxious symptoms and panic episodes, can be useful in the short term, but in the long run generate a strong psychological dependence and, very often, the symptoms of agoraphobia recur to their suspension.*

3- Obsessive Compulsive Disorder (OCD)

Obsessive compulsive disorder is characterized by recurring thoughts, images or impulses. These trigger anxiety/disgust and "force" the person to perform repetitive material or mental actions to calm down. Sometimes obsessions are also erroneously called delusions or fixations. As the name suggests, obsessive compulsive disorder involves the existence of symptoms such as obsessions and compulsions. At least 80% of obsessive patients have obsessions and compulsions, less than 20% have only obsessions or only compulsions. Obsessive-compulsive disorder (OCD) affects 2 to 3% of people over a lifetime, regardless of sex. It may begin in childhood, adolescence or early adulthood. In many cases the first symptoms appear very early, in most cases before the age of 25 (15% of the subjects remember a beginning around the age of 10). If the OCD is not properly treated, first of all with a specific cognitive behavioral psychotherapy, it tends to become chronic and to worsen over time. Obsessions are intrusive and repetitive thoughts, images or impulses, perceived as uncontrollable by those who experience them. Such ideas are felt as disturbing and usually judged as unfounded or excessive. Obsessions with obsessive-compulsive disorder trigger unpleasant and very intense emotions, such as anxiety, disgust and guilt. Consequently, feel the need to do everything possible to reassure themselves and manage their own emotional discomfort. Typical compulsions of obsessive-compulsive disorder are also called ceremonial or ritual. These are repetitive behaviors (such as controlling, washing/washing, ordering, etc.) or mental actions (praying, repeating formulas, counting) aimed at containing the emotional discomfort caused by the thoughts and impulses that characterize the obsessions described above. The compulsions easily become rigid rules of behavior and are decidedly excessive, at times bizarre in the eyes of the observers. Those suffering from obsessive disorders may:

• to fear too much dirt, germs and/or disgusting substances;

• be terrified of inadvertently causing harm to oneself or others (of whatever nature: health, economic, emotional, etc.) for errors, lightness, carelessness, carelessness;

• fear of losing control of their impulses by becoming aggressive, perverse, self-harming, blasphemous, etc.;

• have persistent doubts about their feelings towards the partner or their sexual orientation, although they usually recognize that this is not justified;

• feel the need to carry out actions and arrange objects always in the "right way", complete, "well done".

The symptoms of DOC are very heterogeneous, but in practice we usually distinguish some types. Some patients may have more than one type of disorder at the same time or at different times in their life. Symptoms are obsessions and compulsions related to improbable (or unrealistic) infections or contaminations. "Contaminants" often become not only objective dirt, but also urine, faeces, blood and syringes, raw meat, sick people, genitals, sweat, and even soaps, solvents and detergents, containing chemical substances *potentially "harmful". Sometimes feelings of dirt are triggered even by immoral thoughts or memories of traumatic events, without any contact with contaminants. In this case we speak of mental contamination. If the person comes into contact with one of the "contaminants", or in any case feels a feeling of dirt, he performs a series of compulsions (rituals) of washing, cleaning, sterilization or disinfection. This is in order to neutralize the action of the germs and to calm down to the possibility of contagion or to get rid of the feeling of dirt and disgust. The symptoms are obsessions and compulsions involving prolonged and repeated checks without necessity, aimed at repairing or preventing serious misfortunes or accidents. People who suffer from it tend to control and double-check. This is to make sure that we have done everything possible to prevent any possible catastrophe. Sometimes to reassure yourself about the obsessive doubt of doing something wrong and not remembering it. Within this category there are symptoms such as: having closed your home doors and windows, car doors, gas and water tap, garage door or* medicine cabinet. But also, to have turned off electric stoves or other appliances, the lights in every room of the house or the headlights in the car. Or not losing personal belongings by dropping them or unintentionally hitting someone with a car. symptoms are thoughts or, more often, images related to scenes in which the person implements unwanted and unacceptable behavior. These are meaningless, dangerous or socially inconvenient (attacking someone, having homosexual or pedophilic relationships, betraying your partner, blaspheming, blaspheming, offending loved ones, etc.). These people have neither mental rituals nor compulsions, but only thoughts obsessive. However, they put in place strategies to reassure themselves. For example, they go through the past mentally to make sure they haven't done certain things. Or they constantly monitor the feelings they feel and strive to counter unwelcome thoughts and impulses.

4- Social phobia

The main characteristic of social phobia is the fear of acting, in front of others, in an embarrassing or humiliating way and of receiving negative judgments. Social anxiety can lead sufferers to avoid most social situations, for fear of being "wrong" and being misjudged. Social phobia is a widespread disorder among the population. According to some studies, the percentage of people who suffer from it ranged from 3% to 13%. According to these studies it seems that social anxiety characterizes more women than men. Usually the situations most feared by those suffering from social phobia (or social anxiety) are those that imply the need to do something in front of other people, such as for example to present a report or even just sign, phone or eat; Sometimes it can create social anxiety just by walking into a room where people are already sitting, or talking to a friend. People who suffer from social phobia fear appearing anxious and showing the "signs", that is, afraid of turning red in the face, of trembling, of stuttering, of sweating, of having a heartbeat, or of remaining silent without being able to speak with others, without having the "ready" line. Finally, it often happens that those who experience social anxiety, when they are not in a feared situation, recognize their own fear as unreasonable and tend, consequently, to accuse themselves and reproach themselves for not being able to do things that everyone does. Social phobia, if left untreated, tends to remain stable and chronic, and can often give rise to other disorders such as depression. This disorder appears to begin normally in adolescence or early adulthood. Usually there are two types of Social Phobia:

simple, when the person experiences social anxiety only in one or a few types of situations (for example, he is unable to speak in public, but has no problems in other social situations such as attending a party or talking to a stranger);

generalized, when instead the person fears almost all social situations. In the most severe and pervasive forms, we tend to prefer the diagnosis of Avoidant Personality Disorder.

The main feature of social phobia is the fear of being in social situations or being observed while doing something, such as speaking in public or, more simply, talking to a person, writing, eating or calling.

In feared social situations, people with social anxiety are worried about appearing embarrassed and, above all, are afraid that others will find them anxious, weak, "crazy", or stupid. They are symptoms of social phobia, therefore, fear of public speaking out of concern for forgetting suddenly what you have to say or for fear that others notice the shaking of your hands or voice, or extreme anxiety when talking to others for fear of appearing unclear. The most perceived symptoms of social phobia (related to anxiety) are: palpitations (79%), tremors (75%), sweats (74%), muscle tension (64%), nausea (63%), dry mouth (61%), flushes (57%), redness (51%), headaches (46%).

5- Post-traumatic stress disorder

According to the DSM-IV-TR (APA, 2000), Post Traumatic Stress Disorder develops as a result of exposure to a stressful and traumatic event that the person experienced directly, or witnessed, and which involved death, or death threats, or serious injury, or a threat to your own or others' physical integrity. The person's response to the event involves intense fear, a sense of powerlessness and/or horror. The symptoms of PTSD can be grouped into three main categories:

the continuous reliving of the traumatic event: the event is relived persistently by the individual through images, thoughts, perceptions, nightmares; the persistent avoidance of stimuli associated with the event or attenuation of the general reactivity: The person tries to avoid thinking about the trauma or being exposed to stimuli that can bring it to his mind. The obtuseness of the general reactivity manifests itself in the diminished interest for the others, in a sense of detachment and of extraneousness; symptoms of a state of persistent hyperactivation like difficulty to fall asleep or to maintain the sleep, difficulty to concentrate, hypervigilance and exaggerated alarm responses. The symptoms of post-traumatic stress disorder can arise immediately after the trauma or after months. The picture of the symptoms can also be acute, if the duration of the symptoms is less than three months, chronic if it has a longer duration, or late onset, if at least 6 months have elapsed between the event and the onset of symptoms. Traumatic events experienced directly capable of triggering post-traumatic stress disorder may include all those situations in which the person felt in serious danger such as military combat, violent personal aggression, kidnapping, terrorist attack, torture, imprisonment as a prisoner of war or in a concentration camp, natural or provoked disasters, serious car accidents, rapes, etc... Events experienced as witnesses include observing situations in which another person is seriously injured or witnessing the unnatural death of another person due to violent assault, accident, war or disaster, or being in front of a dead body unexpectedly. Just knowing that a family member or close friend has been attacked, had an accident or died (especially if death is sudden and unexpected) can cause post-traumatic stress disorder. This disorder can be particularly serious and prolonged when the stressful event is devised by man (e.g., torture, kidnapping). The probability of developing it can increase in proportion to the intensity and physical proximity to the stressful factor. The treatment of post-traumatic stress disorder necessarily requires cognitive-behavioral psychotherapeutic intervention.

6- Generalized anxiety disorder

The person with Generalized Anxiety Disorder experiences a constant state of anxiety, often concerning small things and characterized by apprehensive expectation with pessimistic anticipation of negative or catastrophic events of all kinds in nature. In addition to this excessive and uncontrollable concern for any condition, generalized anxiety also manifests with somatic symptoms, such as sweating, flushing, heartbeat, extrasystole, nausea, diarrhea, dry mouth, knot in the throat, etc... Sometimes they are complained about musculoskeletal disorders, such as tension (especially in the neck and neck), tics, tremors, fatigue. Muscle tension typical of generalized anxiety disorder can also be expressed with widespread algic or headache manifestations. Individuals with this disorder are often irritable, short-tempered, unable to relax and even to maintain concentration; they are described as often restless, distracted and impatient people. They often suffer from insomnia and brood over the possibility of impending misfortunes, for themselves and others. Children with Generalized Anxiety

Disorder tend to worry too much about their performance and, in the course of the disorder, the core of the worry can move from one object to another. The disorder - basically chronic and long-lasting - can easily be accompanied by depression and lead to an abuse of alcohol, caffeine, stimulants and other substances. To diagnose a Generalized Anxiety Disorder, the essential feature of the picture - the presence of excessive concerns inherent in most common activities of the subject - must occupy most of the time. The person is not able to control such apprehensive expectation.

In addition, at least three of the following symptoms are required for diagnosis:

Restlessness or feeling "nerves to the waist"

Fatigue,

Irritability,

Concentration difficulties or memory gaps

Muscle tension

Restless sleep, unsatisfactory or difficulty falling asleep.

Behavioral cognitive therapy (among the most effective and highly recommendable) addresses generalized anxiety in different ways. The various situations in which anxiety occurs through behavioural techniques and cognitive restructuring can be dealt with separately. Some use relaxation techniques to interrupt the process of self-feeding anxiety and lower the state of general tension. Finally, we can choose interventions aimed at strengthening assertive capabilities. Among the most common pharmacological treatments for generalized anxiety disorder are certainly those based on anxiolytics. Benzodiazepines are, in fact, the most widely used drugs; however, buspirone is certainly a more recent and equally effective compound. Among the antidepressants with good anxiolytic action are also used Sertraline and Paroxetine.

Chapter II Who Is Panic?

Sudden attacks of anxiety and overwhelming fear that lasts several minutes? Maybe with heartbeat, sweating, wheezing and paralyzed brain. The attack appears suddenly, without obvious reasons, leaving the terror of possible relapses. A panic attack is a sudden episode of intense fear that develops without an apparent reason and that can also manifest itself in the form of physical symptoms, such as:

• accelerated pulse (tachycardia),

• chest or stomach pain,

• difficulty in breathing,

• weakness or dizziness,

• perspiration; and

• feeling hot or shivering cold,

• tingling or numbness of hands.

Panic attacks can be really scary because the patient can be led to think of

- to lose control,

- having a heart attack,

- to be near death,

but generally, they do not pose a physical danger to the organism.

It can strike at any time, anywhere and without warning; essential element for the formulation of the diagnosis is the duration of the episode, which in the case of panic attack must be limited to a few minutes (otherwise they are different conditions, such as generalized anxiety, crisis hysterical, ...).

Once recognized as a form of nervousness or stress, today they are now considered a real medical condition in its own right, which is part of anxiety disorders. If one or two life-span episodes are considered potentially physiological, a higher frequency may be the sign of a possible anxiety disorder, which is called panic disorder (Not all subjects experiencing panic attacks develop the disorder). Panic disorder is more common in women; it usually appears for the first time in young age adults, sometimes when a subject is *subjected to intense stress. Many cases improve with treatment, because therapy can show how to recognize and change the modes of thought before panic breaks out (cognitive behavioral therapy). Drugs can also help. When panic disorder is not treated, it heavily affects the quality of life, because it can trigger other fears and mental disorders, problems at work or school and social isolation. In fact, they can generate the fear of recurrence and lead the subject to avoid places where they have occurred. In some people fear takes over the daily life, so much so that they can no longer get out of the house.*

The disorder sometimes shows a family trend, although there is no certainty as to why some family members suffer and others do not.

Research has found that different areas of the brain, as well as different biological processes, play a key role in fear and anxiety. Some researchers think that in panic disorder the subject mistakenly interprets body sensations as threats and reacts through mechanisms thousands of years old and called fight-or-flight (fight or flight); we think for example of a prehistoric man who is suddenly faced with predator, without any interest in the rational part of the brain the subject would react instinctively looking for escape if possible, preparing for the fight in the absence of alternatives. The organism in this situation prepares for the reaction by increasing the heartbeat to promote strength and explosiveness in the reaction, a typical symptom of panic attacks.

In the case of phobias, for example, we think of agoraphobia panic attacks, behaviors are then declined in two ways:

• fugue (the subject wants to escape from the situation at the onset of the first symptoms),

• avoidance (the subject will tend in the future to avoid places and situations he considers at risk).

The removal from the situation has the effect of rapidly reducing anxiety, but has as a serious side effect that of sensitizing the patient for the future... The improvement of knowledge on how the brain and body work in people with panic disorder will help to find better treatments. The scientific community is also investigating the possible roles of stress and environmental factors.

Symptoms appear for the first time in general in late adolescence (and by 30 years anyway) and are diagnosed more often by women than men. Other important risk factors are:

• family life,

• stress (also understood as mourning, birth of a child, ...),

• past of physical or sexual abuse,

• traumatic events.

When a person is under heavy stress for long periods, he is exposed to the risk of a panic attack; it is estimated that the greatest risk begins after about 6-8 months of tension, but clearly many subjective and external factors take over in this case.

After a time that seems to last forever, the breath normalizes and the fear and thoughts of death disappear, leaving the subject empty and exhausted. These attacks typically occur a couple of times a month; the victim begins to *think they are going crazy. A subject with panic disorder suffers sudden and repeated attacks of fear that last a few minutes; panic attacks are characterized by fear of urgent disasters or loss of control in the absence of real dangers. Intense physical reactions can also appear, so concrete that it looks like a heart attack. Panic attacks can occur at any time, so much so that many people with panic disorder live with worry that they reappear. Panic disorder can lead a person to feel discouraged and shameful about the inability to handle normal routines such as going to school or work, shopping or driving.*

The most characteristic panic attack symptoms are:

• sudden and repeated attacks of overwhelming anxiety and fear;

• feeling out of control, or a sense of death or compelling tragedy during the attack;

• associated physical symptoms such as heartbeat or accelerated pulse, sweating, chills, tremors, wheezing, weakness or dizziness, tingling or numbness in the hands,

chest pain, gastric pain and nausea;

• strong concern about when the next attack will occur;

• fear or circumvention of places where attacks have occurred.

Often the subject undergoing the attack tends to imagine serious explanations regarding the physical symptoms he feels, building fears related to heart attack, stroke and fear of death in general. This attitude has as a consequence a worsening of physical symptoms, with the trigger of an endless vicious circle made of fears and excessive attention to the signals of one's body. That said, since some symptoms may actually suggest life-threatening conditions, it is important to get an accurate diagnosis and treatment. There may be few or many of these symptoms; they usually start suddenly, without warning, and reach their peak within 10 minutes. They last about half an hour, but are however very variable, persisting even of the hours or, in rare occasions, up to a whole day. You may feel tired and worn out after a panic attack has subsided. One of the worst aspects is the intense fear of having another attack. The number of attacks depends on the situation, some patients develop 1-2 attacks per month, while others up to several episodes per week. They can strike at any time without warning: while driving, at school, at work or at the cinema, even during sleep. It is often said that a panic attack is unpredictable and sudden, but in fact in the literature it is possible to identify authors who have investigated more deeply discovering that in some patients it is possible to highlight objective signals that precede the actual attack. The studies are unfortunately limited both in terms of numbers (in terms of participants) and research conditions, but equally interesting in their conclusions; it seems possible that several measurable parameters, for example related to respiratory activity, begin to show alterations almost an hour before the actual attack (regardless of the cause-effect relationship, whose direction might be interesting to explore). Almost invariably patients talk about sudden and unexpected attacks, but it is possible that a psychological approach that takes these aspects into account, by teaching the subject to recognize and deal with them, can be useful to reduce the frequency of episodes.

If not treated, panic attacks and disorders can lead to serious social, family and professional (or school) repercussions, which can significantly interfere in any area of life of the affected person. Some patients develop specific phobias (such as fear of driving), depression and increased risk of substance abuse or alcohol abuse, as well as suicide; note instead that there is an inverse risk, depression does NOT lead to developing panic attacks. In patients where pre-existing heart problems have been excluded, there is generally no direct risk to physical health.

Diagnosis:

All people with panic disorder have panic attacks, but the opposite is not true, so it is important for the doctor and especially for the patient to proceed to a correct and accurate diagnosis, which also excludes certain heart or other problems (e.g., hyperthyroidism, which may cause similar symptoms). The first step is typically a physical examination, which *involves checking vital signs such as*

• heart rate;

• blood pressure; and

• temperatures and temperatures;

and heart and lung auscultation.

When needed your doctor will prescribe blood tests, such as a blood count and the doses of thyroid hormones, while in selected patients you may need an electrocardiogram to rule out heart problems. The next step is the psychological evaluation, usually carried out by a specialist. If panic attacks are not recognized and properly treated, they can worsen and turn into panic disorder or other phobias.

Treatment for panic attacks and disorders is usually very effective and the goal is to eliminate all symptoms related to episodes. The first step, indispensable, is to expose the symptoms to your doctor, who will examine the patient and reconstruct his history, to be sure that there are no physical problems at the origin of the symptoms. The use of a mental

health specialist, namely a psychiatrist or a psychologist, may therefore be indicated. Panic disorder is usually treated with psychotherapy, medication, or a combination of both approaches, but note that the path of resolution is not always necessarily long and suffered, because not all "treatments" predict or require time dilated.

Psychotherapy

Psychotherapy can help to understand the causes of panic attacks and disorders and to identify how to deal with them.

The approach called cognitive behavioral therapy is particularly useful in panic disorder as a first line of treatment; alternative ways of thinking, behaving and reacting to feelings associated with panic attacks are taught to the patient. The attacks will begin to disappear once they acquire different modes of reaction to the physical feelings of anxiety and fear that characterize them.

Medications

Numerous families of medicines are available to treat panic attacks, including:

• antidepressants:

selective serotonin reuptake inhibitors (Ssris),

serotonin-norepinephrine reuptake inhibitors (Snris),

• beta-blockers; and

• benzodiazepines.

The SSRI and SNRI drugs, typically used in the treatment of depression, are also useful on the symptoms of panic disorder. They may take several days to reach full effectiveness and, like all medications, may cause side effects such as

• headache; and

• nausea; and

• difficulty in sleeping.

In general, side effects are not severe, especially if the therapeutic dose is reached gradually, starting from a low dose. Side effects should still be reported to your doctor.

Among the most common molecules we remember for example

• SSRIs

or citalopram (Seropram®),

or escitalopram (Cipralex®),

or fluoxetine (Prozac®),

or paroxetine (Sereupin®),

or sertraline (Zoloft®)

• SNRI

or duloxetine (Cymbalta®),

or venlafaxine (Efexor®).

In some patients, older antidepressant molecules, such as tricyclic or MAO inhibitors, may be used.

Another family of medications, beta-blockers, can help control some physical symptoms associated with panic disorder, such as accelerated pulse. Although usually the doctor does not prescribe them for this purpose, they may be useful in some patients who experience cardiac symptoms.

Benzodiazepines, a category of sedative drugs, are highly effective in rapidly reducing the symptoms of a panic attack, but cause tolerance and dependence if used continuously. The doctor can then prescribe them only for short periods and only when really necessary.

Among the most used we remember:

• alprazolam (Xanax®);

• clonazepam (Rivotril®);

• lorazepam (Tavor®, Control®);

• bromazepam (Lexotan®).

It is of paramount importance not to abandon therapy too quickly, regardless of the approach chosen. Both psychotherapy and drug treatment take some time before they are effective.

Even a healthy lifestyle can help combat panic attacks:

• to sleep properly;

- *regular physical activity;*

- *to feed well;*

- *rely on family and friends of trust.*

A panic attack is characterized by physical symptoms, such as

- *agitation; and*

- *feeling of disorientation;*

- *nausea shall be:*

- *rapid and irregular heartbeat;*

- *dryness of the jaws;*

- *lack of breath;*

- *perspiration; and*

- *dizziness.*

The symptoms are as harmless as they are frightening to those who experience them, triggering fear of a heart attack or even the terror of dying. Most episodes last from a few minutes to half an hour, but even a relatively short time may seem infinite for the affected patient. The most important aspect when experiencing panic is to strive to repeat to yourself that the symptoms you are experiencing are not dangerous and are instead caused only by anxiety; It is very important not to let fear control you and stay focused on rationality and lucidity of thought. Many specialists advise you to face the fear, accept it, to find out and touch with your hand that nothing terrible will happen. It is useful in these cases to have a trusted person next to you, as well as to apply relaxation techniques (yoga, autogenous training, ...) that also provide an adequate respiratory technique; We remember that encouraging the increase of the respiratory rate can cause hyperventilation and increase of the oxygenation of the blood, with consequent worsening of the symptoms, better to strive to slow down the respiration.

Prevention

1. Practice yoga, pilates, autogenous training or other relaxation techniques.

2. Regular exercise, especially if aerobic, will help reduce stress and tension, as well as promote the release of brain neurotransmitters that can improve mood and well-being.

3. A varied and healthy diet can concretely help to manage and prevent panic attacks, for example avoiding sudden changes in circulating sugar levels, a phenomenon that can trigger the symptoms of the attack.

4. Avoid caffeine, alcohol and tuxedo.

MOST COMMON QUESTIONS AND ANSWERS

1- What are panic attacks?

- A panic attack consists of a set of physical symptoms and sensations that accompany an intense state of anxiety and fear that suddenly appears, unpredictably and without a rational cause. The duration is usually limited to a few minutes, but leaves the affected patient the

terror of experiencing the crisis again.

2- Why are they coming?

 - As with many mental health conditions, the exact cause behind the development of panic attacks is unknown, but it is thought that they may somehow be linked to a variable combination of traumatic/stressful events, familiarity, brain abnormalities of some neurotransmitters.

3- How do they manifest?

Possible symptoms of a panic attack include:

• fast heartbeat;

• feeling tired and weak;

• increase in sweating;

• nausea; and

• chest and stomach pain;

• lack of breath;

- tremors; and

- hot flashes; and

- chills; and

- sense of suffocation and/or imminent death;

- dizziness; and

- tingling and alteration of skin sensitivity;

- dry mouth;

- tinnitus; and

- fear of having a heart attack;

- fear of losing control;

4- How long do they last?

- Most panic attacks last between 5 and 20 minutes, but in some cases they may persist for up to one hour.

5- What to do during a panic attack?

- Stay where you are, avoiding trying to suppress the attack;

• *Breathe slowly and deeply;*

• *remind themselves that this is a crisis that will quickly end, with no health consequences;*

• *Focus your attention on positive and relaxing thoughts.*

6- How to cure panic attacks?

- About one in three people will manifest a panic attack in their life, but these are cases that do not require any treatment because they are destined not to repeat; In patients where seizures are more frequent, it is possible that panic disorder is diagnosed, a condition that requires medical assistance. The treatment usually includes a psychological path (for example through cognitive behavioral therapy) and possibly short-term medications; the practice of relaxation and meditation techniques can be of great help.

7- What to take for panic attacks?

- In the treatment of panic disorder medications belonging to the class of antidepressants or benzodiazepines may be prescribed (for example Xanax drops, one of the most prescribed medicines) but these are short-term solutions that can provide relief to the symptoms rather than cure than the underlying condition.

Chapter III Who is depression?

Depression is a widespread and well-known psychiatric pathology. During the depressive state patients feel hopeless and feel a sense of futility, incapacity and despair.

The depressive state not only involves the mood and mind of the patient, but also affects the body, alters eating habits, sleep, self-perception, affective manifestations and the behavior of an individual.

Depression is among the five most common diseases in the Western world and affects 12% of the population. The incidence of this pathology in men and women is in a 1:2 ratio.

Depression can also develop in pediatric and adolescent age, with the incidence of one child in their 50s under the age of 12 and one in every 20 adolescents.

In particular, adolescent depression mainly affects girls, probably due to hormonal and bodily changes that occur in puberty.

Premenstrual depressive syndrome (PMS) and postpartum depression represent other depressive states of the female sphere in which the cause of the disease can be attributed to the variation of hormones.

Depression, however, also affects the elderly. In this category of patients, symptoms associated with depressive pathology are often attributed to a normal aging condition; this can cause a non-diagnosis, resulting in worsening of the disease. In addition, very often, older people are reluctant to express feelings of sadness or despair, which makes it even more difficult to diagnose depression.

In any case, whatever the cause of depression and the category of patients it affects, it is necessary to intervene as soon as possible with an accurate diagnosis and with appropriate drug treatment to avoid the chronicization of the pathology.

There are numerous types of depression, which can be differentiated according to the type and severity of symptoms and the age of onset.

Types of Depressive Diseases

The term "depression" does not indicate a single type of disease, in fact, there are different forms of depressive, each with peculiar characteristics. Here are some of them:

•Unipolar depression or major depressive disorder: this is one of the most severe forms of depression. Its symptoms prevent the carrying out of normal daily activities (for example, sleeping and eating), but also activities that under normal conditions give positive sensations and pleasure.

•Distimal disorder or disstimia: this is a disorder characterized by symptoms very similar to those of major depression, although they tend to manifest themselves more mildly.

•Depressive disorder not otherwise specified: this is a category in which there are disorders that cannot be classified into other types of depressive forms.

•Bipolar disorders or manic-depressive pathologies: these are disorders characterized by the alternation of depressive states to *manic or hypomaniacal states. In turn, bipolar disorders are divided into:*

•Type I bipolar disorder: characterized by at least one episode of mania or mixed alternating with depressive episodes;

•Type II bipolar disorder: characterized by states of hypomania (never mania) that alternate with depressive episodes;

•Cyclothymic disorder or cyclotimia: it has a minimum duration of at least two years and is characterized by the alternation of mild to moderate depressive episodes and hypomaniacal episodes.

How does depression manifest itself?

The symptoms with which depression manifests itself may vary depending on the depressive form of the patient and its severity, not to mention that there may also be subjective variability from individual to individual.

In any case, below we remember some of the main symptoms that can manifest themselves in the presence of depressive disorders:

•Persistent and accentuated low and sad mood;

•Frustration;

•Decrease in interest and pleasure in carrying out any type of activity;

•Low self-esteem;

•Difficulty of concentration;

•Absence of sexual desire;

•Lack of appetite;

•Insomnia;

•Asthenia.

Depression can often be associated with anxiety states and suicidal or self-harming thoughts.

How to cure depression?

The treatment of depression depends on several factors, such as the depressive form that affects the patient and its severity. In addition, the therapy that the doctor decides to put in place can also be varied depending on the patient's response to the same treatment.

In any case, we can say that, normally, the treatment of depression involves a combination therapy that combines a drug treatment with psychotherapy treatment.

The drugs used in the treatment of depression are the so-called antidepressant drugs of which the following classes are part:

•Tricyclic antidepressants (TCA);

•Selective serotonin reuptake inhibitors (SSRIs);

•Norepinephrine and serotonin (NSRI) reuptake inhibitors;

•Selective norepine reuptake inhibitors (NaRI);

•Serotonin transmission modulators (SARI);

•Norenergic and serotonin transmission modulators (NaSSA);

•Dopamine reuptake inhibitors and norepinepine reuptake inhibitors (DNRI);

•Inhibitors of monoamino oxidase (non-selective IMAO and selective MAO-A).

It is believed that the cause of depression is due to the role played by certain types of neurotransmitters. These neurotransmitters are monoamines serotonin (or 5-HT), norepinephrine (or NA) and dopamine (or DA).

In order to better understand the mechanism of action of these neurotransmitters, a brief premise about their physiology is indispensable.

Serotonin, norepinephrine and dopamine are synthesized within monoaminergic neurons. In particular, 5-HT is synthesized into serotonin neurons, NA in norenergic neurons, and DA in dopaminergic neurons.

Once synthesized, the monoamines are stored in vesicles and released into the synaptic wall (the space between the presinaptic and postsynaptic nerve endings) in response to certain stimuli.

Once released into synaptic space, monoamines interact with their receptors placed both on the membrane of postsinaptic nerve termination and on the membrane of the presinaptic nerve termination. This interaction gives rise to a cascade of signals that leads to a certain biological response.

After explaining their function, monoamines bind to the receptors responsible for their reuptake (SERT for serotonin reuptake and NET for norepinephrine reuptake) and are reported within the presynaptic nerve termination.

Once recalculated, monoamines are metabolized by specific enzymes, monoamino oxidase (MAO) and catecol-O-methyl transferase (COMT). In fact, the exact cause of depression is not well known. In this respect, several hypotheses have been formulated:

Monoaminegical hypothesis

According to this hypothesis, depression would be caused by a deficiency of serotonin, norepinephrine and dopamine.

Supporting this theory is the fact that antidepressant drugs increase the transmission of these monoamines.

However, antidepressants very quickly alter monoamine concentrations, but the therapeutic effect is established only weeks later. In addition, there is no relationship between the power of the effect on the extracellular concentration of monoamines and antidepressant efficacy; in other words, it is not said that a drug that can greatly increase the concentration of monoamines in the synaptic wall has better antidepressant properties.

Therefore, it is evident that the deficiency of serotonin, norepinephrine and dopamine cannot be the only cause of depression.

Receptor sensitivity hypothesis

This hypothesis states that depression is not only caused by monoamine deficiency, but also by an altered sensitivity of postsinaptic receptors to these same neurotransmitters. The concept behind this theory is that in patients with depression, serotonin and norenergic postsinaptic receptors have become hypersensitive to their respective neurotransmitters, as a result of their depletion from the synaptic wall. Antidepressant drugs, therefore, would induce a hyposensitivity of these same receptors and this would explain why the therapeutic effect is established only a few weeks after the start of treatment.

Permissive hypothesis

This hypothesis highlights the importance of the reciprocal balance of serotonin and norepinephrine in mood regulators. In fact, if the serotonin level is too low, the norenergic regulation is lost and this can generate alterations in norepinephrine levels. Such alterations can lead to mania. If, on the other hand, it is the norepinephrine level that decreases, the serotonin regulation is lost, resulting in an alteration in serotonin levels. This leads to the appearance of typical symptoms of depression.

Hormonal hypothesis

This hypothesis states that the alteration of the hypothalamic-pituitary-arrenal (HPA) axis may be able to affect the levels of serotonin and norepinephrine released by their respective neurons, thus compromising their functioning. The various hypotheses formulated, therefore, all agree that depression is due - directly or indirectly - to changes in serotonin and norepinephrine *levels. As for dopamine, although its role in the etiology of depression is still unclear, it is believed that it is still involved in the onset of the pathology.*

Although the monoamineergic hypothesis is insufficient to explain why depression develops, it remains the most accredited hypothesis. The monoaminergic therapeutic approach is the most successful and, in fact, most antidepressant drugs act by increasing serotonin and norenergic transmission.

Development of antidepressant drugs

Before 1950, there were no antidepressant drugs as we understand them today. The only therapies used in the treatment of depression focused on the use of amphetamine stimulants or electroconvulsive therapy. However, the use of amphetamine drugs was often ineffective, resulting in an increase in patient activity and energy. Electroconvulsive therapy, on the other hand, although effective, terrified patients because it caused pain. The first antidepressant drugs were discovered in the late 1950s. These drugs were tricyclic antidepressants (TCA) and monoamino oxidase inhibitors (IMAO). As with many of the most important discoveries made by man, the synthesis of antidepressants also came not from design, but from chance. The forefather of tricyclic antidepressants - imipramine - was discovered by Swiss psychiatrist Ronald Kuhn while looking for new chlorpromazine-like compounds to treat schizophrenia. The second major discovery was that of monoamino oxidase inhibitors. Again, the discovery occurred by chance thanks to the development of analogues of isoniozide (nicotinic acid hydrazide), a drug used in the treatment of tuberculosis. The first analogue of isoniazide to be synthesized was hyproniazide. During the clinical trials of this derivative, there was a considerable improvement in mood in tuberculosis patients. However, hyproniazide turned out to be hepatotoxic at the therapeutic doses necessary to obtain both an antituberchular action and an antidepressant action. The discovery of the antidepressant action of hyproniazide, however, gave impetus to the search for new monoamino oxidase *inhibitors. This impulse led to the synthesis of hydrazine derivatives and non-hydrazine derivatives with lower toxicity than that induced by hyproniazide. However, due to the side effects that the first TCA and IMAO inducing - especially at the cardiovascular level - it was necessary to look for new drugs that could increase the monoamineergic signal without inducing such serious adverse effects. In the late 1960s it was discovered that some antihistamine drugs were able to selectively inhibit serotonin reuptake and were cardiotoxicity-free. Since, already with the use of TCA and IMAO it was immediately clear the importance of serotonin in depressive diseases, the purpose of pharmaceutical chemists was to detect and synthesize selective serotonin reuptake inhibitory drugs (SSRIs), with the aim of obtaining highly selective compounds for the serotonin reuptake transporter, but with fewer side effects - or at least less severe side effects - than those induced by TCA and IMAO. The first success in this field was achieved with the synthesis of zimeldine, a derivative of amitriptylin (a TCA). This molecule, in fact, was able to selectively inhibit the reuptake of 5-HT with a minimal effect on the norepinepine reuptake and did not present the side effects typical of CT. Zimeldine was later withdrawn in the early 1980s as it favored the development of Guillain-Barré syndrome. However, the success of zimeldin gave the impetus for the development of new antidepressant drugs. This impulse led - in the late 1970s - to the discovery of many new SSRIs and other antidepressant drugs, such as norepinephrine and serotonin reuptake inhibitors (NSRIs).*

Classes of antidepressant drugs

As mentioned above, the development of antidepressant drugs had a noticeable impulse in the late 1970s and throughout the 1980s. This led to the synthesis of new and numerous molecules.

Tricyclic antidepressants (TCA)

As stated above, these drugs were the first real antidepressants to be discovered. TCOs inhibit the reuptake of both serotonin and norepinephrine, binding to receptors dedicated to their reuptake within the presynaptic nerve termination, SERT and NET. However, these drugs cause many side effects, since they also inhibit other systems of the organism. For this reason, TCAs are referred to as "dirty drugs".

In particular, TCAs are able to:

1-Block muscarinic receptors (antilinegical action);

2-Block α1-adrenergic receptors;

3-Block H1 receptors (antihistamine action);

4-Block sodium channels at the heart level and at the level of the central nervous system.

Amitriptylin, imipramine, clomipramine, nortriptylin, desipramine and amoxapine are part of this class of drugs.

Selective serotonin reuptake inhibitors (SSRIs)

SSRIs selectively bind to SERT, thus inhibiting serotonin reuptake. Unlike TCA they do not block muscarine, adrenergic and serotonin receptors and, above all, are not cardiotoxic. Fluoxetine, fluvoxamine, citalopram, escitalopram, sertraline and paroxetine belong to this class of drugs. Norepinephrine and serotonin reuptake inhibitors (NSRI). As the name itself says, these drugs inhibit the reuptake of both serotonin and norepinephrine by binding to SERT and NET receptors. In a way, TCAs can be considered the precursors of this class of antidepressants. However, NSRIs - unlike their tricyclic precursors - do not block other neuroreceptors and, therefore, have fewer side effects. Duloxetine and venlafaxine belong to this class of drugs.

Selective norepine reuptake inhibitors (NaRI)

Selective norepinepinethrepine reuptake inhibitors selectively bind to the NET receptor, thus favoring a greater permanence of the neurotransmitter in the synaptic wall.

Reboxetine belongs to this class of drugs.

Serotonin transmission modulators (SARI)

Drugs belonging to this class perform their antidepressant action by enhancing serotonin transmission through antagonism against 5-HT2 receptors and through a weak inhibition of the reuptake of the same neurotransmitter. Trazodone and nefazodone are part of this category of drugs.

Norenergic and serotonin transmission modulators (NaSSA)

This category of drugs performs its own antidepressant action by antagonizing adrenergic receptors α2 and antagonizing serotonin receptors 5-HT2 or 5-HT3. Mirtazapine belongs to this class of drugs.

Dopamine reuptake inhibitors and norepinethrenaline (DNRI)

These drugs selectively inhibit dopamine reuptake and - to a lesser extent - norepinepinepine. They can also exercise mild inhibition of serotonin reuptake. This category of drugs includes bupropion, a drug used not only in the treatment of major depression but also in smoking addiction therapy.

Monoamino oxidase inhibitors (IMAO)

As their own name states, these drugs act by inhibiting particular types of enzymes, called monoamino oxidases and related to monoamine metabolism. Two MAO isoforms are known, MAO-A and MAO-B. Drugs used to treat depression are non-selective MAO inhibitors - such as phenylzine and tranilcipromine - and selective MAO-A inhibitors, such as moclobemide. Selective MAO-B inhibitors, on the other hand, are mainly used in the treatment of Parkinson's disease.

Mood stabilizers

Mood stabilizers are used to treat bipolar disorder. They can have both acute and long-term effects. The best known mood stabilizer is definitely lithium carbonate.

Herbal therapy

Herbal therapy can also be used for the treatment of mild to moderate depression. In particular, it refers to the treatment of depressive pathology with Hypericus, otherwise known as St. John's herb.

This plant, in fact, is able to inhibit serotonin reuptake just like SSRIs, but, in addition, it is able to increase norepinephrine levels, resulting in increased energy and responsiveness. Finally, hypericon is also able to increase dopamine levels, thus promoting an increase in the sense of well-being.

What to do

It is not always easy to distinguish a "difficult period" from the actual depressive symptoms. Early diagnosis is very often hampered by shame and rejection of this condition. Below we will list some useful tips to recognize a depressive symptom and suggest how to intervene. It is necessary to prevent the consolidation of symptoms and the aggravation of the pathology by making an early diagnosis. Depression often begins with some simple maluments, apparently "physiological", although more intense, repeated and close:

1-Negative perception of events.

2-Sadness and irritability.

3-Feeling of "depression" (it is used to call it such, but this word is very often used inappropriately, while tending to oate it when the doubt is stronger).

In this first phase it is very important to try to reverse the mood trend as a preventive action. If untreated, these symptoms can evolve into a frankly clinical condition and determine the appearance of:

4-Depressed mood throughout the day and for several days.

5-Inability to feel pleasure during normally fulfilling activities.

6-Unjustified or excessive irritability, negativity and emotional pain.

7-Anhedonia (tiredness, fatigue, lack of energy).

8-Abnormal increase or reduction of appetite.

9-Sleep disturbances.

10-Slowing down or motor agitation.

11-Lack of concentration.

12-Feeling of failure, guilt (own or others) and futility.

13-Tendency to isolation.

14-Recurring thoughts on suicide.

The most important diagnostic aspect is the pervasiveness of the symptoms (i.e. constancy and duration), but it is not said that they all manifest themselves at the same time.

Having suspected of suffering from a depressive disorder it is necessary to consult a doctor immediately:

Gp for the first approach: usually prescribes light drugs to facilitate spontaneous remission.

Specialist: psychiatrist or neurologist. It is able to more accurately identify the type of disorder and prescribe specific therapy.

Therapist: psychologist - psychotherapist. It identifies the psychological mechanism that causes mood disorder and intervenes by modifying mental paths, processing system, etc. It does not prescribe drugs.

That said, some very important tips for prevention (at the first symptoms) and also for treatment are:

1-Do not abandon customary activities.

2-Attend the community.

3-Adhere to a balanced diet.

4-Practice sports motor activities.

5-Do not abuse psychotropic substances: alcoholism, drugs, smoking, binge eating disorder (compulsive feeding).

6-Avoid only circumstances that really cause suffering.

7-Dedicate yourself to interesting activities and able to "disconnect the brain" from the brood (continuously thinking about the future) or from the thinking continuously about the past.

8-Abandon clichés, try to overcome shame and seek help in times of need. By addressing a specialist early, in most cases you can solve the problem with light interventions and without leaving too significant experiences.

Ultimately, the main remedies are:

•Psychotherapy.

•Drug therapy.

•Combination of both.

What NOT to do

1-Give up an early diagnosis by not turning to your doctor.

2-Stop the diagnostic process if your GP recommends a specialist visit.

3-Underestimate recurrent mood and negative attitudes.

4-Give in to anhedonia and stop most activities (work, sports, hobbies, social relations, etc.).

5-Neglect sleep and do not regularize it.

6-Neglect the diet.

7-Isolate yourself.

8-Brood and ruminant continuously.

9-Avoid or discontinue drug therapy.

10-Avoid or discontinue psychotherapy.

11-Abuse of psychotropic substances.

12-Strive for self-harm and strive to deal with particularly uncomfortable circumstances.

What to Eat

The food role in depressive pathology is controversial.

There are scientific bases that suggest a correlation, but the real impact is not always so significant (see also: Diet and Depression: prevent it at the table).

In general, it is recommended to:

1-Adopt a normocaloric and balanced diet. Sometimes it requires special effort, since some drugs used in the treatment have an anorexic effect.

2-Respect a diet with the right fraction of carbohydrates.

3-Hypoglycaemia and a possible ketoacidosis caused by fasting or a low carb diet alter mood, creating a "swinging" pattern.

4-Hyperglycaemia caused by a diet too high in carbohydrates can lead to a decrease in glucose use by brain tissue, confusion, slowing down and lethargy.

5-If welcome, take a portion of coffee when waking up in the morning (worst time in the depressed); can improve mood, as long as it does not interfere with pharmacological action.

6-Promote the consumption of foods rich in omega 3: they guarantee the integrity of neurons; so also their functionality. They are abundant in fishery products, in certain oilseeds (flax, kiwis, grape seeds, soybeans, etc.) and related oils, krill oil, cod liver, etc.

What NOT to eat

1-Avoid low-calorie diets, as they increase the risk of worsening symptoms.

2-Avoid excess drinks, supplements and strongly stimulating foods such as: coffee, tea, energy drink, cocoa, dark chocolate etc. It is especially important in bipolar disorders, tendencies to abuse and clinical frameworks also characterized by anxious symptoms.

3-Avoid taking alcoholic beverages: increase the risk of abuse and adversely affect drug metabolism. They can make anhedonia worse.

4-Avoid foods very rich in histamine: it has a stimulating action that can impair drug action or trigger severe headaches and worsen anxiety. It is present especially in fishery products (blue fish) and increases significantly with bad conservation.

5-Avoid foods very rich in thymine: it is a derivative of the amino acid tyrosine. Like the previous one it is a marker of poor preservation. Stimulates the release of norepinepinethylene by predisposing to tachycardia, headache, etc. It abounds in cheeses, preserved meats, soy sauce, fish, red wine and other spirits, bananas and chocolate.

6-Avoid foods very rich in glutamate: it is an amino acid that acts as an exciting neurotransmitter. Widely used in the food industry as a flavor enhancer, it abounds in broth nut, ready-made or icy soups etc. Excess is very difficult to achieve with diet, but it can happen in Chinese cuisine.

7-Avoid excess cholesterol and saturated or hydrogenated fats (especially in trans conformation): they do not have a direct negative effect on depression, but a diet rich in these molecules is associated with a worsening of brain function. They abound in junk foods such as fast food, packaged, fatty cheeses, margarines, bifracted oils etc.

8-Avoid excess arachidonic acid: it is an omega 6 derived from linoleic acid. It is abundant in some oilseeds and related oils (for example, in peanuts and extraction oil). Especially when associated with an omega 3 deficiency, the arachidonic acid exuberance seems to worsen brain function.

9-Do not follow diets without carbohydrates or with too many carbohydrates.

Chapter IV: How does those who meet monsters live? How is it seen by others?

As mentioned above, more and more people have unfortunately had to deal with these terrible monsters at least once in their lives. Many wanted to leave witness to their experiences to encourage those who meet this type of beast not to be ashamed, not to hide, not to barricade themselves in the house for fear of not being understood but to let themselves be helped to find the best way out; but at the same time it literally sucks those who judge, those who criticize, those who have unfounded prejudices, those who do not even know where the word empathy and sensitivity is on the dictionary.

1-Carolina, 25 years old tells;

I suffer from very strong anxiety attacks: I'm always afraid something will happen. My anxiety unfortunately manifests itself with a series of physical disorders: cold and acidic sweat, frozen skin, heart-pounding, inability to concentrate and keep myself lucid, tremors, desire to take absurd actions to solve the theme that triggered my anxiety. I'm always afraid that something is going to happen or something irreparable has happened, that someone is dead or in danger, that there are no solutions to solve all my problems, and that everything will collapse inexorably without me being able to control it or do anything to stop the fall. My anxiety also prevents me from facing a few days: going to do blood tests can become very complicated if I have to make sure I'm in the office right after that. It doesn't matter that I took a regular permit for prenatal exams, anyway I'm going to get anxiety and end up procrastinating the tests. My anxiety spoils my sleep: I wake up at night thinking that I have to do washing machines, clean the bathroom, pay my bills, solve a banking issue and make the memory of the show "La Locandiera". The anxiety I feel sometimes prevents me from going out in the evening because I fear something may happen to my loved ones while I find myself unable to reach them promptly in case of need. This condition made me live the first few weeks of pregnancy very badly: at the first two ultrasounds I trembled and the doctor could not take the pressure until I saw my baby's heartbeat on the monitor. Anxiety generally makes it difficult for me to maintain control in times of high stress at work, only over the years have I learned to manage times of crisis forcing myself not-so-well-as to keep my cool. Sometimes I'm so crazy that I have anxiety because I'm afraid of anxiety. Sometimes it ends very badly and I find myself at the mercy of real panic attacks where I think I am there to leave our pens. What do I do to get better? Nothing to date. Unfortunately, I am no longer in analysis for an infinite number of reasons, every now and then I feel the need to go back, but then I give priority to things that seem to me to be more important. I try to put into practice some old teachings to stem the problem, but there are some themes that drag me into the darkness and cold of my tremendous unconscious. The death of my loved ones is one of these themes: if mom, Claudio, dad or one of my brothers does not answer the phone I immediately think that it may be in danger or that it is already beautiful that passed to better life. This leads me to make compulsive phone calls one after the other, because if the person on the other side of the phone does not answer me immediately I really risk making me all of Rome on foot to find it. The whole thing intensifies if we are covered by moped, bicycle, car. Sometimes I'm sick, sometimes I'm sick, sometimes I'm fine: it depends on stress and tiredness. The more pressured they are, the more anxiety and irrational thoughts will appear. Once, at the Colosseum, I wrote a message on Facebook to a guy who was then a complete stranger to ask him about the movements he had made with Claudio, who was late for the appointment, with his cell phone off, and was generating in me yet another crazy attack of anxiety. I looked like a jealous psychopathic girlfriend, i was actually afraid Claudio was dead. If I'm ashamed? Yes, I'm ashamed, especially when *in the grip of total irrationality I do things that might make me think of bad things. I can pass for jealous girlfriend, hysterical girlfriend, dictator girlfriend ... In the course of my life I have been hung many, but the truth is that mine is true fear. I need to be reassured that everything is in order, that everything is going as it should go, that there is nothing dangerous or wrong. I need the message when you get home and I need the message when you leave to come back to me. Today Claudio is in a woods filming for a short film and his mobile phone does not take. He doesn't get any messages or phone calls. All day, all night and all day tomorrow. I'm home alone, I'm going to sleep alone, and tomorrow morning I'm going to wake up alone. I used to pay for a similar condition, now I'm here trying to come up with ways to spend the night without succumbing to anxiety. I thought I'd unveil this little insight into my personality because I'm sure I'm not alone, I'm sure a lot of people like me suffer as well as I suffer, fighting every day against a monster that doesn't exist and can't kill us and that in fact it's not even dangerous. I believe that this awareness, that of not being the only one, could easily be the first step towards a definitive resolution. However, the best way is always to ask a specialist for help, these situations often have their roots in unresolved issues of the past, or in disequibooks that should be investigated from a medical point of view. The analysis helped me a lot, but I almost always had the impression that a definitive resolution did not exist, but that there were only strategies to stem and keep the disorder controlled. The comparison I think also serves to disprove or confirm my resigned vision. It wasn't easy to write and share these four lines, but I think it's useful for those who think they're alone. I think it's necessary for me because, writing lover, black-on-white things make me less afraid.*

2-Francesca, 47 years old says:

Francesca looks like this. "The problem is that I worry too much, of everything. I have no reason not to worry about anything. Work, family, health, my dog. Everything makes me anxious. Maybe I should say I care about everything that makes up my life. I realize I can't stop worrying. I cannot say or decide not to worry for a certain period of time, or at a certain time. Like when I go out with friends, or to sleep. I'm constantly worried about anything. This thing is ruining my life, I'm not relaxing, I feel like I'm going crazy, i'm not in control anymore! I don't live, if not my worries. They put all my time and energy into it." Francesca makes us understand how generalized anxiety represents a state characterized by excessive anxiety and worries, intrusive and pervasive, that compromise the entire life of the person who suffers from it. It expresses the perception of a total lack of control over its concerns, another characteristic element of generalized anxiety. "This has been going on for years. I have been living these thousand concerns and fears for years. I worry so much that I get tired, I feel tired and without energy. Maybe at times I'm depressed and exhausting. I'm often agitated, tense, so tense that my muscles hurt, irritable, I can't focus, not even on what my boss is telling me, if that's when my worries started. I now call them, by name, "my concerns." Then, when I'm lucky, stomach ache begins, atrocious cramps begin. My fiancé says that the lack of rest, in fact, my inability to rest and my insomnia worsen everything I feel. These problems started gradually, and became unmanageable."

Francesca describes the typical symptoms of generalized anxiety: easy irritability, restlessness, feeling tense or with nerves on the skin, easy fatigue, lack of rest, difficulty concentrating or empty memory, muscle tension, gastro-intestinal disorders, insomnia or agitated sleep. Francesca often describes her brooding, a process that can be described as chains of negative thoughts that increase and maintain the state of anxiety that triggered it initially, creating a vicious circle. Simple muzzle is not a specific trait of generalized anxiety. We can all experience it in our lives. What mainly differentiates the pathological expression of brooding are the poor perceived control over it and the insofance, despite several attempts, to reduce it. "I feel powerless in the face of my concerns, it is as if in their presence I cease to exist, I block my life, everything I am doing at that moment, to give space to them. I tried to turn on the radio, read something, call a friend. It initially worked. For a few moments I could shift the focus away from my worries. After a while, a sense of compulsity creeps in, as if what I started to do in order not to listen to my concerns was no longer a distraction, but an element of disturbance. So I'm starting to hate what I'm doing, not to put up with it, to realize that it's not what I care about. Who do I want to give her a drink to? I can't help but worry. I can't help but worry. And I come back to worry, more anxious and defeated, incapable, powerless than before." "Sometimes I think that worrying in this way I'll go crazy. I'm going to go crazy. How can I think of living like this, of spending my life worrying like this? one fine day I will go crazy, in the midst of a concern of mine, totally impossible to reassure and modify. Maybe at that moment

I'm going to stop worrying, or maybe I'm going to be a very worried madwoman. When I think about these things I feel totally at the mercy of my thoughts, I feel that my attempts to block them are in vain. And anxiety, as well as worries, increase." In this case Francesca makes a "negative" assessment of her constant concerns. He judges them as dangerous as they could lead them to madness and madness. At the same time he experiences the failure of his attempts to distract himself and suppress the brood, or to avoid certain situations for fear of not obtaining satisfactory results, or to ask for continuous reassurances from other people reinforcing his belief that he cannot control his concerns, that he is powerless and that he risks going crazy at the mercy of these thoughts, considerably increasing his anxious state. According to the cognitive-behavioral model, the constant concerns of the person with generalized anxiety disorder, and therefore the thinking continuously to the past, can become the subject of even positive assessments, as people experience these assessments as the only possible way to "keep under control" their problems, to feel prepared *to face or to prevent the tragic expectations that are expected. This belief is wrong because, paradoxically, maintaining high levels of anxiety and continuing to worry, the symptomatology described above exacerbates and maintains the anxiety disorder itself is accentuated, according to a vicious circle. The result is that the mind is more occupied in brooding. These processes, when recurrent and systematic, lead to psycho-physical suffering.*

3-Paola Perego says:

She calls him the Monster. Paola Perego began to suffer panic attacks at the age of 16, when they were not yet known and the most that a doctor said was "she has a nervous breakdown". They tormented her for 30 years until, mainly thanks to cognitive behavioral psychotherapy, she stopped "being afraid of fear". Did he defeat the monster? "It took me 30 years, but for about ten years it has. Psychotherapy was fundamental, in the third I won the battle. The monster was part of me, it is part of me for everyone. With therapy you experience your defects, emotions, needs and, when you really know them, it is no longer scary. The cause is always much less frightening than the panic attacks it generates. For years, for a living, I had to take medication."

But she managed to build a career. It must not have been easy.

"I could not drive, not go out, not eat, not see my friends. But never stay without work. Because I needed it to live and because my father gave me a very strong sense of duty."

His son also suffered. Did it help him?

"I was very agitated. In the book there is a drawing of him describing an attack. He wanted to come out early. I was telling him, am I going to pick you up? And he'd get back in the car on his own. It was very strong. He had therapy and in a year he came out of it."

How was your husband Lucio Presta close to you?

"He understood me. We must never say: it is nothing, or willpower is enough. He never judged me, made me feel inferior, weak. He stood next to me and distracted me. Lucius is a very solid man: whatever may happen, he calls a helicopter and rescues you.

4-Sabrina says:

I suffer sporadic panic attacks from the tender age of 19; or rather, at the age of 19 this thing was "officially diagnosed" to me, but I think I have always suffered from it. Now I am 34 years old, the time and the various seasons of life are taking their course, but my "faithful friends" in all these years have almost never abandoned me. I have been better in pregnancy, although in pregnancy you cannot take specific drugs if not in minimal dose, but panic attacks are part of my existence and come back to see me when I least expect it, often when I am about to forget about their existence. This is their way of existence, perhaps, and maybe it's mine too. In my path I have often found myself next to people who have no idea what it means to live with this *pathology, or that this is precisely a pathology in all respects. Some stayed and wanted to know, understand, others remained silent and in acceptance, but many, many, escaped, joining my feeling of panic the sense of abandonment that only makes things worse. I, meanwhile, have realized that this "disease" is much more widespread than you might think and that it is often the most unsuspected people who suffer, those who are perhaps always ready to listen to others without email complaining, to be strong when no one would be, to get up in the morning without almost having slept and go to work without making a turn. Often, it's those people you feel you can lean on, because they're as strong as rocks and you can't catch a glimpse of this darkness inside, if you don't know it. The complete darkness, this is a panic attack. A feeling of fear, death and abandonment totalizing and uncontrollable, which takes your mind and paralyzes your body. The first time he came to see me was a scorching August afternoon and I began to feel a tremendous cold on my way home, a cold that produced a tremor that found no relief in anything, blankets, Phon and* sweatshirts. I was leaning against the wall crying and shaking, but shaking so hard that my heart and all my bowels were shaking too. I was thinking of a very dear person who recently disappeared and in a moment his death was mine. Who was supposed to do anything did his best and that's how I met Mr. Valium and then Mr. Xanax and all the other respectable gentlemen who still keep me company on the grayest days. What happens during a panic attack? It happens that you are no longer you, that you perceive yourself as a stranger trapped in a body and a mind that you have absolutely no control over, that you need to go you do not know where, to run away from you do not know what, to stop the tremor of your legs and hands you do not know how. It happens that the walls seem to bend, the voices distort, the sounds mingle if not for the most annoying noises, which amplify; it happens that you are suddenly alone and helpless while maybe you are in the middle of a supermarket with hundreds of people and it seems to you that everyone can see what is happening inside you. It happens that for a few moments you die and then you are reborn, *exhausted as those who fought a battle against the most atrocious of enemies and with the world that did not fall, but that went very close to us. I have been asked many times how I can live with panic attacks and at the same time be a mother, work, be a wife. The truth is that those who suffer from panic attacks are not necessarily different from you normal people, if not in those moments when you completely lose, that if you know them panic attacks become an enemy to live with and to give up softly when possible, because only then can you hinder it the moment when you cannot tolerate that you necessarily want to take with you. I am not a psychologist or neurologist, but I can say that only a long therapy has allowed me to understand where these black holes come from in my case and above all how not to succumb. I had sporadic or frequent panic attacks in any situation in my life, even while giving birth to my daughter, during important business appointments while talking in front of more or less people, while parading on the catwalk in my early twenties, while shopping with my little girls, simply while I was asleep, waking up suddenly with this feeling of death. I have always survived and few times have I really lost control; Today I recognize the panic attacks from the tremor to the hands that distinguish them in my case and when I really have to try to neutralize them, to ask them for a small extension of a few minutes or a few hours, to hide their hands that tremble and take a big breath. When I'm alone and I can afford it (so very rarely) I stop rejecting them and let myself die for a few minutes, sure I'll wake up stronger than before. Last year, when I first heard the song En and Xanax by Bersani on the radio, I smiled and even today I listen and listen to it again and i sing it again... And that's exactly how I think: "if you don't get scared with my fears, one day you tell me yours we will find a way to remove them". I am one who shamelessly lives with fear and those who do not want to understand this fear or simply those who are not able not to be frightened, cannot be part of my life path. I think my little girls know that too (although I obviously never explained to them explicitly what happens to me in those dark moments, limiting myself to saying that "Mom is tired and must rest for a moment")...*

They know it, because when I sink into the dark they stroke my back and stop as if by magic to fight or ask questions. They know that their mom from the dark always comes back and that it's just a matter of moments where you have to give so much more love, or just if you can't keep quiet next to you. Ask yourself questions, ask yourself questions, be indiscreet, but never leave alone a person who suffers from this disorder, because probably her sensitivity will lead her to be one of the best people you will be lucky enough to know in your life.

5-I'm a 19-year-old boy, my name is Ben and I've never been happy. I divided my life into four parts:

a) 3-10 years: weight gain phase and beginning of the awareness of being "different".

b) 10-14 years: chronic phase, full adolescence, where I suffered physical and psychological torture from the people around me and the first social discrimination at every level. loneliness. Weight gain.

c) 14-17 years: psychological change, regularized bad habits (alcohol, smoking), progressive increase in aggression and discouragement of living, emotions of hatred and complacency in seeing the suffering of others, loss of a year of school due to my bad performance, increased pessimism, beginning of loss of self-esteem. More weight gain.

d) 17-19 years: stabilized bad habits, stabilized an aggressive and vindictive personality, imbalances and mood swings, chronic pessimism, weight loss due to hospitalization, grumpy, double personality, surrendered to life, false, malignant and recently mentally unbalanced.

Always obese, never had a girl, I have always had difficulties in clothing, discriminated against and mocked by everyone. Now I ride with a trekking carabiner in my pocket in case I find me in trouble in the face of any dangers and have to use it as a knuckle-knuckle-knuckle to vent the anger of 19 years of life without ever smiling.

6-Since she was a child, it sounds crazy, but it is. I remember isolating myself and crying thinking the same thing all the time: "No one loves me." Now I'm 40 years old and my life has always been a swing of more or less conscious illnesses. Yet others think I'm a strong woman, always smiling, "so sunny" they tell me. The only way I can feel good is not to get emotionally involved. But it is not always possible and when it happens (in work, in affections, in family relationships) and I live even a slight disappointment, it is a disaster. I think I'd better not be there, not live, let it all go. I was from two different psychoanalyses, one working in a public hospital and one private (from one euro per minute) but, encouragement aside, they could not point me out. I also followed a medication treatment, especially to be able to sleep, which made me feel better, but when I suspended it (after three months) everything came back exactly as before. I am sure that I will come out of it, as has happened on other occasions, using reason, making myself guided by rationality and common sense, distinguishing what is right from what is wrong. I have to take my heart off, though, and live coldly because, if I let myself be overwhelmed by feelings and passions, I remain disappointed, I am sick and crying, I do not sleep, I do not want to live. Who knows, maybe those who said, "But idiots, why don't they suffer from depression?" are right. Maybe that's just the case, like having blonde hair or crooked nose, maybe depression is not a disease, but it's the crooked nose. Sometimes I think I just need not to be alone, to live as i used to be in the community, all together with grandparents, cousins, relatives and neighbors, a simpler and poorer life, but perhaps richer in humanity. Despite everything, I still hope...

7-For five years I have faced countless difficult times: university, economic difficulties, road accidents of my loved ones (one after the other), loss of my best friend (she did not die, but she deeply disappointed me). I was going ahead with my teeth tight because there was the goal: to graduate and do a job that would reward me (for this and only for this reason I had found the strength to face university). After school I find a job as a receptionist... boring work. Countless interviews: only unpaid internships and I couldn't accept them, I needed money. So, here's the bitter discovery. For eight nights I didn't sleep, with the nightmare of having to go and do a job I hated. Hallucinations, guilt that led me to a psychotic crisis: the vivid feeling of being in hell, with screams from the demon. Luckily for me there was my brother who forcibly took me, shouting at me to trust him... well I trusted and from hell I went to heaven. I've been there and there's nothing in the world like that feeling of infinite love. anyway... they hospitalized me and after two weeks of psychodrugs I returned to life. Then more relapses, because bore boreness gripped me and I didn't know what to do in life. I gave myself to my only passion: dance. It was real therapy for me... but if I have to tell you all about it, the decisive step to get out of it was the deep acceptance of the disease. The moment I indulged her, she stopped hurting me and I found a taste for little things. Now I'm going to go to dance school, I have a lot of friends and also a new best friend. I'm back to life. I'm back to love. Hope people... if I made it, you can do it too. A kiss to everyone. I love you.

8-My name is Daniele, I am 23 years old and I have been suffering from depression for about five years. I write probably because having to declare that you are in depression is already something. It sucks everything, I no longer love life, I feel absent (a tissue), I hate people, I have become over the years very naughty and airy, I no longer have good feelings: this at least is what I think. At the end of my mind, however, I am good, but my character is hard and intransigent, I go out little at home because people do not stimulate me and now I have everyone on my balls: they have no idea about anything, they live their insulting lives without knowing what suffering is. That's my problem: I suffer and I don't know why, I go to the doctors, I take medication, but the most important thing right now is that life sucks at me. To others so much and to me shit to pull down every day, to others normality and to me suffering. Surely it's the depression that made me that way. I can't say I've had panic attacks, but the mood has been under my heels for a long time and whatever I do I feel won over by life and unable to enjoy it. The good things are there, but if you can't live them, what's the point of life? Anyway, you have to try to react, but how? I don't know if you understand me, but the biggest evil is helplessness. In life or you are there, and then everything is still ok or you are not there and then they are bitter cabbage. Lack of love: in addition to the damage also mockery. Greetings to all

9-I'm 40 years old and in my life I've always had to fight. My father, an elderly and alcoholic, did not give me security or help in any sense, indeed, at the age of 16, due to his car accident, in addition to studying I also had to take care of his small farm. Despite my insecurity, I was the best graduate of the school and my employers always appreciated me for the efficiency and ability to solve problems. In interpersonal relationships, perhaps because of my introverted and a little shy character, I always suffered, but I masked my insecurity with activism and being always on the move. In 1992, in three months, I practically lost both my parents, but I didn't come down and react. I have always worked and in the short time off I took care of the small farm. Despite the initial difficulties, I managed to build a house and achieve, at the cost of enormous sacrifices, a small economic security. This year, in the spring, also because of demanding work and perhaps always to be in the running, anxiety crises began. In early June I collapsed morally and physically and went into depression. I felt inadequate, self-esteem was under my heels, I didn't want to eat or do anything and my head got lost in bad thoughts. I immediately turned to a specialist who helped me, even with medication, to get out of that negative moment. My wife, my in-laws and the few friends who understood my problem are helping me. Now, after two months, I've started work again, I know I'm not completely out of depression and some days are really hard, but I'm learning to accept myself for who I am and to consider that in my life I've also done something good. Sometimes, in fact, I think depression has made me realize that you have to live life guilt-free and without excessive wear and tear. To all the people who are in this situation I say: we can get out of it, we are different from the others because we are more sensitive, but this negative experience will make us stronger.

10- I recently realized this, since I publicly asked for help, but deep down I knew that my way of loving was not right and that the more I loved the more I suffered the more I suffered. I also came to think about getting it over with: I didn't want my life to continue with that suffering. Then I stopped. I relived the last few years in a flash and was ashamed of myself and what I had done. I met him by chance, after seven happy years of marriage and a daughter, and he came into my life. I was flattered that such a brilliant man, full of commitments, looked at me. I was overweight, dressing like a tomboy, and yet I guessed he was interested. It took him a few words and in just six months I lost 15 kg (I didn't eat anymore) and changed my look. I listened and followed his every word and little by little I fell in love. But for him an extramarital affair with me was not good (even if he had had others). Every time we had intimate relationships, the next day he accused me of pushing him to cheat on his wife. And so the years have passed, I always by his side at work, supporting him, supporting him, sacrificing my life and career for his, hoping *that one day he could change and be able not to feel and not make me feel guilty about this feeling. Needless to say, it has not changed, indeed it has now also moved away. I haven't seen each other for some time: I miss him immensely, but I'm much stronger than before. Now I use the energies for me, to move forward and no longer for him, to please him, to live up to every situation, to be brilliant, nice, friend, lover and confidant. Now I feel anger towards him. He always managed to keep me on a leash and if I tried to get away, he could bring me back next to him. I talked about it with experts, going into much more detail than can be done in a few lines, I cried and I felt compassion for me, they said to me "She suffers from Affective Addiction": too bad however that they were not able (public structure of Milan) to take charge of me, so day after day I learn on my own and write, remember and cry.*

11-I'm 44 years old, at least 30 of whom have been suffering from depression. I first felt the first ailments around the age of 13/14, but maybe I was suffering latently from them before. I remember that my gp, a general practitioner, had diagnosed me with "neuro-vegetative distonia" perhaps in the absence of a better term, but he could neither give me a cure nor direct me to a specialist. I was suffering from anxiety, although I didn't know it then, and crises increased after my grandfather's death (1979). The following year my father also died and my already rather poor reaction skills were permanently compromised. I also had the misfortune to live in a not-so-friendly environment (family included) since not only did no one help me, but I was even teased and this increased my suffering. My life was totally compromised: I didn't have a girlfriend, no stable job, no social life. Panic attacks forced me to go to the emergency room a couple of times, but no one ever told me my evil was treatable. From 1996 to 1999 I was prey to anxiety, completely addicted to the Lexotan (90 drops a day) that I now self-scribed. In 2000 the turning point. 8

February 2000 to be exact. Despite the deep suffering, partially asleep by benzodiazepines, I found the strength to move to Florence for work. I can't explain why, maybe changing cities and meeting new people, including Deborah, to whom I probably owe my life. From that date I became aware of the evil that had plagued me for a long time and that in practice had literally swallowed my existence and I ran for cover, contacting a psychologist. Psychotherapy on a weekly basis for almost four years, in addition to the intervention of a psychiatrist to eliminate addiction to Lexotan. I slowly recovered the desire to live, the sexual stimulus and the desire to do the things I like to do the most. I've never felt that way in my life. I've held on to a lot of difficulties and 90% of them are out of it. I clung with all my might to the opportunity to heal because I almost immediately understood one thing: you can get out of it.

12-I am 34 years old and I am a mother of two wonderful children. After five years of marriage, my husband and I decided to have our first child who, moreover, did not wait. The pregnancy was splendid: no physical problems and everyone's attentions turned solely on me and my belly! fantastic! Finally comes the long-awaited moment but, contrary to my expectations, I have to submit to a caesarean section. This is the first major disappointment followed, immediately, by the second: the little one does not want to know to stick to my breasts so I am forced to breastfeed him artificially. The world seems to fall on me, I feel like a failed mother and the child I wanted so much now appears to me as a bulky presence! I cry all the time, a sense of deep anguish accompanies me throughout all the days that, moreover, seem interminable to me, I am bequeas the idea that my life will never be more that of before, that I will no longer be able to take care of my things because now I am the mother of a little stranger who is totally dependent on me! With my husband I can no longer communicate, it seems to me that he is not able to understand me; The only person I want next to me is my mother because I know that she, too, has suffered from depressive problems in the past. On his advice I turn to a specialist and start a psychotherapeutic path. So I find that so-called postpartum depression affects about 80% of women and, I have to say, this information is a little heartening. Personally I did not need to take medication, but I managed with psychological support to face the difficulties that, initially, seemed insurmountable to me. Today Andrea is almost six years old and his little brother two. Every day with them and for them I learn to be "mom", every day they teach me to appreciate life.

13-I'm 26 years old and I'm in a tunnel that I can't get out of anymore. I've always had great results at school since my early years of university. For the studio I gave up many things, setting aside feelings and entertainment. Then a period of psychological instability began: my repressed homosexuality manifested itself in a disruptive way and led me to a difficult path of physical and ethical self-acceptment. Now I have accepted my nature, I am happy to be like this and I am neither afraid nor ashamed of my way of life. In that period my university results were less brilliant: now I have managed with difficulty to take me to just one exam from graduation, but my average has dropped and the sense of frustration with the results obtained has been added to the lack of interest. And also, I have a tearful anxiety for my last exam, which I have been trying for several months now without being able to overcome, caged as I am in a mixture of inadequacy, fear and stretcher. I lost the combativeness I had in my early years of study and the desire to live my life. Like I've already sold it all out. Recently it has got even worse because my friends are all graduating and starting to enter the world of work, while I have stayed behind everyone. I'm starting to feel a deep malaise even just to leave the house, to be with who made it and who can boast a job, a practitioner or some other stimulating experience.

I would like to cut things aside by setting aside the university for a while and get a job, but I'm afraid I deeply disappoint my parents, who never made me weigh anything, have always been very understanding, they have also accepted my homosexuality, but below they hope that this son will one day give them great satisfaction. The spectre of failure is increasingly present and ever closer. I don't know what to do. I have a wonderful guy that I'm very much in love with, but I can't help but think that his esteem for me may one day fade due to my professional failures. This situation leads me to think that I am less intelligent than the others. Although I have studied a lot and know many things, it is not from notions that mental acuity is measured. I'm always on who goes there. If there's a confrontation, I think the others are right and I'm wrong. My boyfriend is very close to me and knows my *hardships, at least in general, but I'm afraid he'll step away if my constant frustration continues. Mine is not so much afraid to be alone, but to lose love because of me.*

14-Hello. I'm Leila, and I discovered depression six months ago, when I had a boyfriend, went to college, had wonderful friends and family... I never expected that. In fact, it was difficult for me to recognize her: I began to suffer from inappetence, nausea, vomiting, little concentration, but above all I was much and more and more tired. At one point I almost started giving up and spending all my days in bed crying. I consulted a thousand specialists (gastroenterologist, internist...) and to do a thousand tests because I thought it was a physical evil, but it was not so. After two months I started doing psychotherapy and taking antidepressants. After a thousand side effects I stopped crying and slowly started going out and returning to my normal life. After three and a half months of therapy, I feel more confident, more energetic, but I still feel depressed because I can't concentrate on studying anymore. Does anyone know if this depends on depression? I feel useless because my life doesn't go on anymore, because all the plans I had for my future regarding work and love have vanished. The only good thing is that I started studying myself to figure out what I fell on and it's weird how a superficial like me has become so analytical. Only now can I appreciate the simplest things, take myself less seriously and enjoy life more. I found out I had beautiful friends next to me who put up with me all the time and listened to me. Through my confidences we have also managed to become more intimate and more complicit. I have noticed that everyone, more or less visible, more or less seriously, has small big problems. Now they're the one who's calling me to let off steam and ask me for advice. I would like to tell you never to lock yourself in, to have the courage to talk about it with your loved ones or with the people you have just met. Everyone can give you advice and words of comfort because they will trust you that they have also passed us and will not make you feel alone. Never be ashamed because you're not the only ones. Now I am much more sensitive and I am not false if I tell you that I love you and I am close to you because I know what it means... sooner or later we will return as before... even better than before... One kiss.

15-My adventure with this "disease" probably started from childhood, but I don't want to go that far. I'm just telling you, I've had several years of psychoanalysis and i've had a particularly busy life, even though I'm only 41 years old: a separated son from the age of eight, married the first time at 23, the second at 38. Two children from their first marriage, who left with their mother this summer, returning to their native city (500 km away), despite the relationship I had with them. But I don't think that's the root cause of my illness. The current situation is this: in December 2005 I arrived in a state of depression so that I could no longer do anything. I remember at the time I had my parents at home: both they and my wife were seriously worried. During the period of psychotherapy (from 23 to 35 years, for the duration of the first marriage) I used

Tavor at a dose of 3 mg per day. Probably the doctor who treated me did not think I needed antidepressants, also because their use was not part of his method of treatment. Let's say the Tavor was almost my choice, as I realized I was particularly anxious. For about a year I interrupted the sessions with the psychoanalyst i was treating, since he, for family reasons, had been forced to leave the city where I lived. I went to another analyst, also from the same school as the previous one. At one point I decided to stop taking the Tavor (after 17 years), as it seemed like slavery to me: it was quite a difficult thing, but I succeeded. Since then, my behaviour with family members and at work has worsened: I found it difficult to work in an office because it caused me a state of oppression. I was diagnosed with gastroduodenal ulcers, iatale hernia and reflux gastroesophagitis. I often suffer (and still suffer) from manias of persecution: I mentally move from one "culprit" to another, probably because my unconscious seeks an external cause, a responsibility. But I often realize that it is I who makes situations worse myself, to the point where the contrast actually happens. Going back to Christmas in '95, I decided to go to a psychiatrist to submit my case to him, after an unnecessary attempt by my GP to treat me with a minimum dose of Zoloft (50 mg per day). The psychiatrist pointed me to a change of therapy, prescribing me a 75 mg dose of Efexor, plus a mood stabilizer that, in fact, I never took, after reading the package leaflet. The fact is that the cure worked, only that at first I slept a few hours a night, waking up often at 4 or 5 in the morning, with a great desire to do 1000 things. Within four months I resumed a more regular sleep, but the antidepressant effect was increasingly reduced, leading me to decide independently to double the dose: 150 mg of Efexor with prolonged release, in a single dose the night before bedtime. At this point it took effect, but after only two months the improvement vanished again. Probably without Efexor I would be much worse off, but the depression, as described on your site, has returned, along with the manias of persecution. I admit that many times I can recognize that I am the one who distorts reality, but that is not enough to make me feel better. I also did a long period of meditation (about 3 years) which was sometimes effective, sometimes not. Then I stopped. The symptoms are: poor desire to do anything, lack of enthusiasm, apathy, feeling of making a useless life, not being able to have dreams for the future, desire to lock myself in the house and not see anyone, negative thoughts about what others think of me, perennial sense of inadequacy, especially at work, malaise in the presence of many people, difficulties in relationship with others in every situation of my daily life , tendency to close myself in and not tell anyone what goes through my mind (but maybe this is better, given the negative thoughts I do). Frankly, I think it's more of a biological fact than a real psychological fact: there have been a lot of cases of depression in the family, in particular a cousin tried to take her own life and my grandmother committed suicide. I think there's a hereditary component. I see other depressed people in the family who do not care, because they do not want to recognize the problem: I, unlike them, perhaps thanks to therapy, probably accept it more, although with great difficulty. I would need support to calibrate drug therapy: I got tired of living a life in half, always struggling with my malaise. On the other, I am not going to go to psychological therapy again: I have done too much of it and, moreover, I have spent exorbitant amounts.

16- Hi, my name is Kikka I am 24 years old and I suffer from panic attacks... My attacks are a consequence of a depression that began at the age of 15, then when everything seemed over to me, when everything we say had passed me (with the help of some friends) anxiety presented itself.

It literally ruined my life, I missed so many years of my life. In 2009 I had one of my panic attacks due to a fight I saw. From that moment every time someone fought I started shaking and feeling sick... not knowing what I was meeting I went out freely but every day my friends had to accompany me home because I was not well ... I had reached the point of not being able to leave the house because I did not see myself outside the house but only inside, in *front of the TV.*

By 2010 all this had calmed down a bit, I was starting to go out, even though the crowded places I could only see from afar. I thought my life was adjusting and i wasn't... On July 4, 2011, my friends and I decided to go to the beach like all 19-year-olds do. How beautiful, the year before I hadn't missed it once, I was happy to go... I start to get into the water and everything affixed, while I was swimming suddenly something rises from my stomach and does not make me breathe... my friends luckily noticed because I then screamed that I was not feeling well and immediately they took me ashore, they made me sit down I calmed down but nothing to do, so I decided to call my father to pick me up and while I was waiting for that feeling came to me again and I was not breathing ... worried in the evening I went to the medical guard and there the doctor told me that it was anxiety, from that day I stopped living, for fear I also took away the vice of smoking.

At first I went out, then I closed and there was no way to get me to open... I couldn't go on the moped because I was missing the air, I couldn't get out because I was sick... I was really sick, the pain in my chest, the pain in my left arm, the breath I was missing... I was really sick, I missed everything, for this reason I could not go to the sea (I who am olive of complexion I had turned white)...

If I went to the maximum once a year with my aunt and I had to know if there was anyone I could trust, I missed the parties, the outings with friends, the outings with relatives, the sea, the sun, the fun, I never went out with a guy for fear of feeling sick, I made confirmation but in church I started crying because I was sick and when I went to take the course I had to have the it's a little open and sometimes I either didn't go or I had to be together with someone ready to escape, believe me I saw it ugly, even just having coffee with friends for me had become a feat and I don't tell you the highway, my mom, in the car I felt like I was dying, because I always missed the air, and when I miss the night I could suddenly rest in the middle of the night screaming that I could not breathe ...

I started eating worse than a turtle... i really got to a point where I either did something for myself or I would give up... then people didn't understand, as long as they said or said it was or that they too had panic attacks but not like mine... if I just think about what I've been through, I've seen it ugly, I really don't wish it on anyone misses my worst enemy to live like this. I decided to go to a psychiatrist, since Anyway I did not want to take medicine I told her, but I did not see it suitable that I did not know anything about what her work was but besides saying that I had to go out, I had to see the friends did not tell me anything more and therefore even with the sessions I had paid I left ... after years I spoke to my aunt and she advised me a psychologist who worked where she was... and in October of 3 years ago I started going to the psychologist... I have to bless her, I had a problem, I was sick but really that I felt like I was dying, really that I had pains, head turns, stunners, crazy beat, I lacked the air and this was the thing that scared me the most... now I can say that at the age of 24 I am fine!

I am proud of myself and where I arrived

without taking medicines but only taking valerian for a few months and going to the psychologist, the results can be seen at a glance. The others point this out to me too, and I'm really happy about that. In 2014 I went to Paris, which was my dream as a child, I did my first tattoo, I went to the sea a couple of times, although I had my moments because I can say that until summer started I was sick, I did other tattoos including a writing in a foreign language that means "Resist"... this "Resist" gave me the strength to resist never letting go, if I was sick I have to resist that everything will be fine... it's strange you know, before I was looking for security the help in people instead I realized that help and security I have to take in me, I learned to control panic attacks starting to accept them, they are still part of me ... but how good it is when you start to feel sick that really seems to you that you are dying and after a few minutes understand that you are fine and then start telling yourself, next time it comes, to wait because it will pass, everything will pass... This year I did 2 weeks in June at sea, I took a holiday in Puglia with a friend, I went anywhere, I am *dating my friends, I spend more time with them, when i am made a proposal I hardly accept, I go down almost every day to get coffee, after years I enjoyed the feast of the patron saint of my country and the festival that really is an exceptional thing, and to think that people come from all over Italy and also from abroad and I did not go there, in November I will go to the concert of my idols, and finally in 24 years of life I will go out with a boy ... A dear friend of mine told me That I am becoming like when I was little, that is, tanned... let's say I took almost all the things I did before, I took my life back into my own hands... I'm not 100% but I'm almost there and I'm happy about that, because as I slowly thanks to psychotherapy I'm starting to heal everyone can do it... please let yourself be helped, and you must not be ashamed of having anxiety, never cease to be yourself... you are strong, you are brilliant, you are yourself and there is you can do it, at some point in life comes a moment where you say "Enough!" enough to everything you start living again. Get up and live! Sorry for the outburst but what you will do tomorrow does you credit, because everyone thinks that it is nothing, that it is only in our head, but I have seen on my skin that it is not so, anxiety must be experienced and then told, now I want to live, to discover new things and to recover all the years lost in my life ... that's my story, #Niente#Panico !!!!*

KIKKA MARTORELLI

17-Marina says: "It happened in the summer, more than twenty years ago, at the time of university. I was on a bus, heading to the sea: I wanted to spend the day at the beach with a friend. I started to feel sick, I felt suffocated, I had the feeling of fainting and I felt my heart beating too fast. I was terrified and didn't understand why. It was my first panic attack. I ran off the bus and came home hoping it would pass me by. My boyfriend was with me at the time: he too knew absolutely nothing but fish to catch. After a while I was taken to the emergency room: I thought there was something wrong with the heart, because it was beating too hard. They visited me and immediately gave me a calming: I realized that my heart was fine and that the problem was another. Since that day, for several months, I have had violent panic attacks almost every day, and even when I hadn't lived them I lived in terror that they could come any minute. Every situation posed a threat: crossing a bridge, entering a supermarket, taking a bus. I realized I was dealing with a complex problem that was difficult to solve, and so I turned to a psychiatrist who advised me to start psychotherapy. Slowly, slowly, as time went on, I began to understand how I should behave with this disorder. I realized that I could handle the panic attack, that there was no need to rush to call for help and that I could learn to calm down on my own. I would lie down, take an anxiolytic and just wait. I said to myself: 'You just have to wait for it to pass, just wait for it to pass'. I imagined I was in a rough sea and told myself That I just had to "be dead", float on the waves until the storm calmed down. Panic attacks feed on your fear: the more you fear them, the more they come back to see you. When I realized that there was nothing to be afraid of and I began to consider them only as annoying disorders, no more serious than a migraine, I got less and less. Until it disappears altogether. I was free of it for over ten years, but then towards the end of 2012, the problem recurred. It was a difficult time in my life: I was facing several difficulties, including severe mourning. This time anxiety manifested itself in a slightly different way: panic attacks were rarer, they came only at night. But I lived hostage to a thousand different illnesses: tachycardia, tingles, shortness of breath, dizziness, nausea, soft legs. It's called generalized anxiety disorder, a kind of meaningless daily hell. Again, after excluding organic problems, I chose psychotherapy, but with a different awareness. Turning to specialists is certainly important, in many cases necessary, especially when this is the first time this problem has been confronted. However, in the end, the truth is that a 'cure' in the sense of the word does not exist. Panic attacks are often treated with psychotropic drugs, but they do not always work. Psychotherapy can be useful to review your experience and clarify what is happening. But all this is not enough, or at least it was not enough in my case. I kept *getting sick, with symptoms of generalized anxiety throughout the day and a few panic attacks at night. At that time I looked at the situation from a different point of view. I took a period of leave from work and started to deal only with my health. I did yoga, mindfulness meditation, outdoor walks. I realized that to get better I had to review some things in my life that weren't going as well as I would have liked. That's where I decided to write. Writing has always been my passion, but over time I had given it up. So I started studying psychology and self-help books, on anxiety issues but also on psychological well-being in general, and I started writing about what I learned on a blog. Writing has always been important to me. In a way it is a form of meditation: you focus on your thoughts, you make them flow on the sheet. Writing helps to untie a lot of knots, to distance ourselves from our experiences, to rework them. Just buy a notebook and write a little every day, carve out a quiet space for yourself. I find it very therapeutic. After the blog, came up with the idea of writing a book. When I started getting better and went back to work I thought I'd* write about my experience. I wanted to tell what it's like to live with this burden, without victimism, but by explaining well what anxiety and panic attacks are. Unfortunately, there is a communication problem on these issues: many people think that these are unimantic disorders, nonsense that can be overcome with a little willpower. Still others are afraid, because they are mental disorders and on this there is still a strong stigma. We are not used to treating mental health as part of health in general. It seems normal to us to take care of our bodies, but the idea that the mind can also have problems and needs to be kept healthy is still not part of our culture. All this, however, only makes the situation worse for those who are ill. You already have anxiety and panic attacks, then you also feel the mistrust of those around you, the lack of understanding. Then you end up being ashamed, and so you're sick twice: anxiety and shame risk feeding each other. That's why I wrote this book, which is called The Boiled Frog. A story of anxiety, panic attacks and change. To process my story and stop ashamed, and for others to recognize themselves in my story and perhaps *feel less alone. If I were to give advice to a person who is suffering from panic attacks for the first time, I would say above all two things. The first is: learn to face them. They're horrible, they're very scary, a terrifying experience, but in the end they can't really hurt us. When you stop being afraid of it and take care of yourself and your malaise with sweetness and understanding, then you create a breeding ground for panic to come to see you less and less often. Second tip: Ask your GP, specialist, psychotherapist for help. Help is needed. But do not delegate your well-being to these figures, try to understand what are the cares that are proposed to you, informed and choose. And also try to understand what's good for you, what you need to get better. Making movement and cultivating a creative activity for me have been a real medicine".*

18-Ivan tells: I write on tiptoe and with a lot of humility, how I managed to overcome panic attacks, depression and so on. I make this premise because I don't want to teach anyone anything. I don't want to look like a wise guy or what a train knows about it... I'm willing to answer questions and help, but I always do it with a lot of humility. then... one summer afternoon, I was on the sofa at home and all of a sudden, I started to feel my heart beat harder. There I didn't really notice, but the mind wouldn't stop thinking about the beating heart, so I went out for a walk. Nothing, not even that. I go to the parish, I start playing and for a while it seems like it's going through. Then, all of a sudden, he attacks me with all the force he's capable of. Dizziness, tachycardia, soft legs, nausea. Everybody stop! From that day, my end began. Little by little, I was more and more afraid to go out. Going back to the places where I had the attacks then it was unthinkable. I couldn't stay in crowded places anymore (I used to go to university and drop it off), I couldn't make a bus stop, I had to get off right away, especially when the bus was full. And woe betide you to show that I was sick, woe! I was trying to hide everything. In the house, things were even worse. I could no longer eat, to sleep alone (I slept with mom in bed), I had lost weight and was even afraid to laugh (you never know that I could break some vein in my stomach), I slept almost every morning and I no longer played volleyball (I had started at 6 years old and it was the great love of my life). I mean, I didn't live anymore. One day I'm going to sit on the windows window of the balcony thinking about getting it over with... but I didn't have the courage. One morning, my second mom (my maternal grandmother), brought me some weekly (Today, People, etc.) and on one of them, I read the story of Annalisa Minetti, the blind singer. When she learned she was going to go blind, she said she had to choose whether to live or die. And he chose life. Here, I read that sentence and... I don't know how and I don't know why, in my head something came out. I started a slow, but steady ascent. I started devouring books about psychology, self-esteem, and so on. I went to a psychiatrist (only once, but it was enough, because it saved my life), who gave me doses of serotonin and a few drops of calming, but in very low doses. Little by little, I recovered my life. But let's be clear, it wasn't easy at all. I had to get to such a low point, that I never thought I could go back up. Faith was also VERY important. But most of all, it was the character I had, that helped me not to give up, not to abandon myself. It took many and many months, but in the end, I won. I was so passionate about this, that I decided to study medicine and surgery, to be able to help people who go through these dark paths. Here, below I would like to give you some tips that you will surely already know, but you never know:

1) You do not die of panic attacks or anxiety. you don't die. no one has ever died. they are devious and cowardly attacks, but you do not die;

2) Don't be ashamed to admit to suffering from panic attacks. it is a liberating thing to admit it and tell those close to you. do not stifle your mood or anxieties. be yourself;

3) The secret is in the mind. She commands everything. Body follows mind, as well as anxiety and so on. Starts all from here.

Manage it and you will have solved 80% of the problem;

4) Although long, you must never, ever, ever give up;

5) You have to do a reset of your life. Erase everything that happened before the panic, turn you back on and start again. It's a kind of rebirth. You have to forget all the rules you learned, clean up your brain and finally start living, at any age it's never too late.

You're going to have to have a great, but really big willpower. Now, without presumption, I feel much stronger than before. It was the best thing that could happen to me. I say this now, of course, but I swear that overcoming something like this can only give you strength.

I don't know how long it takes to heal, each case is different, but I can tell you that if you want, you really want it, it comes out. I'm living proof of that.

Chapter V: How do you defeat monsters?

Are you looking for remedies for anxiety because you can't really make it anymore? Know that you are not alone, quite the contrary. Defeating anxiety is the crusade of our time, a battle that becomes holy war since it would like to defeat the worst enemy of contemporary man. If you suffer from anxiety and stress, often accompanied by side disorders such as insomnia and inappetence, then you have to run for cover. What? Making you help from the right dietary supplements, as well as of course doing exercise, meditation and reserving a daily parenthesis for yourself. To help you find the right supplements that will cheerful and maybe eliminate your anxiety altogether, we have selected the best products. All natural and free of side effects, safe to take for a psychophysical well-being that will make you reborn. Anxiety is the worst travel companion there is. Since travel is life, let's get it out of the way as soon as possible. So here are all the most valuable anxiety remedies *on the market. Remembering, of course, that in the event of major attacks the correct thing is always to consult a doctor. Matt's Calm Stress is a dietary supplement in drops that can mitigate anxiety. Passiflora promotes relaxation; Valerian is valuable to promote sleep in the presence of stress; Hawthorn has beneficial relaxing effects; The Tiglio promotes relaxation in times of greatest need. This phytofluid combines these four plant principles which, acting synergistically, can be a valid help in times of increased tension and stress. It is recommended to take 20 drops of product twice a day, diluted in a glass of water, possibly away from meals. The product is suitable for vegans.*

•Ansie Stop is Healty Fusion's dietary supplement in 30 capsules that calms anxiety, ideal for all those who are subjected to high levels of stress or great physical or mental effort. It relaxes the nervous system and provides a sense of well-being that leads to a state of relaxation, also necessary to reconcile a quality sleep. formulated with high purity

and quality components, microencapsulated to achieve optimal assimilation. Contains hops, passiflora, louisa grass, L-tryptophan, vitamin B3, B6 and B1.

•Rescue Remedy is the famous blend born from the combination of 5 of the original 38 Bach flowers, namely cherry plum, clematis, rock rose, impatiens, star of bethlehem. Supplied with a 20 ml dropper bottle, it is recommended to take 4 drops directly into the mouth at close intervals until the state of anxiety improves. There are those who blindly believe in Bach's flowers and those who consider Rescue fresh water. Certainly, the content of grape alcohol (the main ingredient used to store flower extracts) will calm you down anyway, so it's also good for skeptics. Perhaps the calming power of Bach's flowers depends precisely on their alcohol content, who knows.

•*CBDoliv is a phytotherapy product extracted from Hemp and endowed with numerous beneficial properties for the body. Made entirely in Italy with 100% natural ingredients, it is free of toxic substances. It has a 10% CBD concentration and also contains numerous Terpenes and Flavonoids that make it a complete, extremely effective and wide-ranging product. Certified and analyzed by the Department of Pharmacy of the Federico II University of Naples, it is produced by Hemp Phytomedical, a leading company in the botanical and phytotherapy sector. The 100 mg CBD/ml is diluted in olive oil. It will effectively allevie anxiety naturally, try to believe.*

•*MAGNESIUM →Magnesium is one of the most important minerals for our organism, because it is involved in the most important reactions of our well-being. Deficiency today is more common than is thought; one of the symptoms is anxiety. Magnesium has a relaxing effect on the nervous system and, if taken regularly, also improves sleep quality.*

•ESSENTIAL OILS →Once you appreciate essential oils and include them in your daily life, you can no longer do without them. Their benefits are many, many of which are also recognized by science. To relieve anxiety and calm the nerves the most suitable are those of chamomile, lavender, ylang ylang, jasmine, lemon balm and cypress. You can use them in a diffuser or even dilute them in a carrier oil for massages. In case of sudden anxiety attacks, massage a few drops on the solar plexus. It will calm your nerves almost instantly.

•OMEGA 3 →The benefits of essential fatty acids are known. They also protect against depression from anxiety. According to one study, students who took 2.5 mg of essential fatty acids for 12 weeks showed less anxiety before an exam than colleagues who had taken a placebo.

•ABSTINENCE FROM THE DIGITAL WORLD→Some studies dated 2010 carried out at the Medical Organization of Hadassah, Israel, show a link between internet addiction, depression and anxiety. But it's not the only documented case, unfortunately. Even some UK research has been able to relate anxiety and technology (computers, mobile phones, social network portals) and reveal that in those predisposed to anxiety, the second acts as a turning point, but makes the person more insecure and more overwhelmed by it. More in detail, this is perhaps best demonstrated by Chinese research based on the study of MRI scans of the brain that highlights that internet addiction can cause brain changes similar to those observed inside the brains of alcoholics and drug addicts, going so far as to show that being addicted to the internet could be the exact same thing that being addicted to cocaine. It's very impactful, right? But that's the way it is and it's proven by science. There is no doubt that information overload, wide choice of technology devices, and emotional engagement of social media can create anxiety as we try to keep up with the digital barrier.

The trick is self-awareness and having willpower. You need to know when it's time to pull the plug.

•VITAMINS →Does that sound strange to you? At first, I admit it too. Then I read a study carried out at swansea University in Wales, which showed that people who took a multivitamin pill for the duration of a month experienced an anxiety reduction of around 68%. This is because they have managed to integrate any deficiencies in the diet and these cause a decrease in the functionality of enzymes which, in turn, can affect moods. vitamins and minerals, therefore, come to the rescue and regulate the biochemical processes in the brain that affect mood. In support of the above-mentioned research comes a second most recent study, dated July 2013, by the University of Calgary that found that vitamin and mineral supplements can improve mental energy and generic well-being in people prone to anxiety. Try to integrate them into your diet and discover its effects, you may be amazed in a positive way!

•TRAINING AWARENESS →An extraordinary tool that we carry with us from the moment our brain functions are complete, is free will. We have the choice of where and when to focus our attention: in things that have a positive impact on us or in as many things that cause us a state of senseless concern. Rick Hanson, a neuropsychologist and one of the most prolific and authoritative authors of the New York Times, describes in his book "Just One Thing" this dual faculty of decision-making as a reflector of combinations that functions as a modern vacuum cleaner: does it reflect thoughts and then suck them? literally inside our brain. What we may not know is that we can train our attention and develop better control over it. Hanson advises and talks about awareness, to train one's mind to exercise awareness. It is scientifically proven that exercising awareness causes the development of cortical layers in regions of the brain that control attention in order to achieve better focus. It also increases the activation of one of the areas of the prefrontal cortex that helps control and reduce negative emotions that can

cause anxiety. But how can we be more aware? Hanson himself recommends taking a few minutes or more every day to practice mindfulness meditation and focus on the sensations that our breath gives. During the day we try to stabilize ourselves and reflect on what is happening around us and within us. You know, you can even use recurring events like meals or a ringing phone to train awareness.

•*HAVING STABLE SOCIAL TIES* →Extensive and rich research shows how high the influence on our long-term health is of the quality of personal relationships and social support. Concordia University researchers say this with a study published in June 2013 in which they reveal that running for cover seeing other people during a stressful event is an effective way to improve mood. Isolating one another, on the contrary, increases anxiety, the risk of depression and decreases confidence in others. Prevention is not a useful strategy as remedies against anxiety. Instead, it is to fortify one's social bonds in order to strengthen one's ability to manage anxiety.

•LISTENING TO MUSIC→Several studies show that listening to music is one of the most powerful and powerful remedies anxiety. It is the scientists at the University of Kentucky who point this out, showing how effective music is as effective as a real non-pharmacological intervention and is able to reduce anxiety before surgery and then relieve physical pain after the surgery to which you have undergone. Now, if music has this great power and can make a strong contribution to fighting anxiety in extremely difficult times in life, let's try to imagine what it can do in everyday life. This is because with music comes a charge of dopamine, the chemical of well-being. Studies show that slow and sweet music is best suited to soothing anxiety.

•FOLLOW THE EXAMPLE OF TIBETAN MONKS→again, I'm not advising you to become a hermit and get away from the chaos of the city. But every scientist and enthusiast of Zen meditation techniques knows that meditation reduces anxiety and there are even

scientific studies that demonstrate its effectiveness. One of them comes from Wake Forest Baptist Medical Center and was published in recent 2013. This research identified which areas of the brain are activated and deactivated during the relief that meditation produces against anxiety. There is more and more talk of conscious meditation in which just a few minutes of practice are enough to reduce the anxiety that is felt in everyday life. In fact, researchers have found that this helps to suppress anxiety by 39 percent. Not bad, isn't it?

•OVERCOMING ANXIETY BY LAUGHING AT IT→It may seem like stupid but it is not. This is what Karen Lynn Cassiday, clinical psychologist at Chicago and President-elect of the Anxiety and Depression Association of America, says. The well-known professional states that cultivating a good sense of humor and laughing is good, even to overcome anxiety. In fact, even it is a fake laugh, not felt with the heart, you release dopamine which is a brain chemical that controls feelings and feeling of reward and pleasure.

A study published in 2008 in The Faseb Journal and presented at a medical conference featured researchers at the University of Loma Linda who discovered how a cheerful laugh is able to reduce cortisol, the stress hormone, which increases when entering the anxious state.

•*GOING TOWARDS SOMETHING THAT YOU CAN TOUCH WITH YOUR HAND*→When anxiety strikes, one of the most useful and productive remedies is to do something concrete. John Tsilimparis, a therapist and marriage and family counselor in Los Angeles and a professor in the psychiatric branch at Pepperdine University, tells us. But what does that mean? What exactly do you want to tell us? More precisely, Tsilimparis suggests grabbing an object and holding it as long as possible, such as an ice cube. And why? The doctor explains that our brain cannot and cannot be in two places and places at the same time, so the activity we are doing distracts us from anxious feelings. The mind will then shift from the catastrophic thoughts that accompany anxiety to the cold ice cube you're holding. According to some research, the Tsilimparis technique is used in a similar way within medical studies. Many doctors, in fact, use a virtual reality distraction system that can reduce anxiety during dental procedures. This study shows that patients immersed in a realistic computer-generated environment reported less anxiety and pain than those who did not.

•PLAN TIME →It seems that carving out a piece of your time every day to worry can be a useful strategy. This is demonstrated by a study carried out in the Netherlands which analysed how people with adaptation and anxiety disorders who programmed 30 minutes of space with themselves to think about their anxieties were then able to cope with their problems. Did the research use a technique called? Stimulus control? and has been analyzed, deepened, studied in detail for a period of 30 years. Therefore, setting aside half an hour of one's day to think about the concerns that are begging us, and thus considering solutions in this regard, makes sure that you avoid returning to it during the rest of the day.

The study was published in the July issue of the Journal of Psychotherapy and Psychosomatic and we will now go to analyze it in more depth.

One Step at a Time: The study began from a base of 62 patients and already observed good results. It turned out that people who used worry reduction techniques before starting therapy regimen reduced symptoms of anxiety, stress and depression, more than those who only use standard treatments. There are four steps involved in stimulus control therapy to reduce anxiety. This is stated by a doctor who was not involved in the research itself but was part of the initial group that developed the therapy in the early 1980s. Firstly, patients will go and identify and realize what they actually feel concerned about. Secondly, they will have to set aside a certain period of time and find a suitable place to think about those anxieties that they have identified. The third step is to capture the moment when you feel anxious and postpone it, focusing your mind on the activity (see the ice cube faced at one of the previous points in the article). Finally, patients will be told to use the time they have carved out to worry and try to solve the problems present in their lives. In the Dutch study, even those who performed only the first of the four suggested steps fared better than those who received only treatment for anxiety disorders, although of course it was worse than those who completed all four stages of therapy. This shows that the stimulus control program is effective, especially if followed after learning how to manage stress.

Trying to Move on: The results raise the idea that some treatments can be more effective if you help afflicted people pass over their concerns a little bit. For this, some doctors indicate that the study should be repeated using large groups of people as samples, thus increasing its overall scope. Because worrying too much can also have a detrimental effect on physical health. But it is possible that excess *anxiety is treated and treated with techniques similar to those that are used to curb overeating. Some examples? People who tend to overeat are advised to set a time and place dedicated to food. In this way, those who eat in front of a television programme can, over time, come to think that watching television can trigger the process of hunger. In the same way, anxious people may find themselves associating the places chosen to worry about the anxieties themselves from which to go to take refuge in the future. This is what the study shows with the facts. However, as with many other treatments, it is enough to prove that the technique itself provides a kind of placebo effect that helps people treat with anxiety. What is well established, however, is that planning a moment to reflect on one's anxieties actually helps to reduce concerns in the long run.*

•FINDING A QUIET PLACE →When a panic attack occurs it is good to retreat to a safe and quiet place, possibly away from people. Crowded places, with the multitude of people

and noises, increase the feeling of malaise. Many lament the sense of compulsity and the fear that "air may not be enough". Others may feel uncomfortable getting noticed by other people, fearing they will be considered "sick" or worse "crazy." If you can, untie your belt or take off your tie to feel comfortable.

•DO NOT GIVE IN TO AVOIDANCE →retreating to a secluded place during the panic attack does not mean having to avoid crowded places a priori. Do not associate the context in which the episode of panic first happens with its cause. There are people who have the first attack on the cinema and stop going for months, others have it in the car and give up driving. There is no link between place and anxiety. In fact, if you avoid all the places that you consider dangerous, all you will do is feed the vicious circle of anxiety, ending up finding yourself alone and locked in doors.

•*RATIONALIZE THOUGHTS* →*Panic attacks do not cause harm, do not lead to death, nor trigger heart attacks. These are anxiety-related manifestations, so you know the cause very well. Although the symptoms are really bad and unpleasant, you have to repeat that they will pass soon and that nothing bad will happen to you. Thinking on the contrary that you may be in danger will only fuel anxiety and consequently encourage all symptoms.*

•*CONTROL BREATHING* →*You can learn to breathe properly rather than follow the breathlessness. Slowly inhale with your nose, imagining inflating a balloon inside your stomach. Hold the air for a few seconds and then throw it out forcefully, deflating the imaginary balloon. To be able to become familiar with breathing techniques it can be useful to follow a course of relaxation and guided imagination. These exercises help reduce anxiety if practiced consistently and will come in handy to understand how to deal with a panic attack.*

•*LEARNING TO RECOGNIZE PANIC ATTACK*→*Paradoxically you will have to become experts in your symptoms and body sensations. This will increase the feeling of being in full control and will not make you fall into fear. Consider that the episode of panic attack has its beginning, a symptomatic point of maximum explosion and then the slow degrowth. This means that the time frame is limited and that you already know what to expect. Repeating these steps to you mentally will reduce disorientation and drive away negative thoughts.*

•*TAKE THE SITUATION INTO YOUR HANDS*→*If you have had a first episode of panic, do not wait for the second one to arrive after a few days or a few months. Your body is sending you a clear message and it's good to understand what it means. Pretending nothing, minimizing and trivializing is not a good answer. When you have a sore throat, don't you usually run for cover? If you notice a caries don't go to the dentist right away to avoid the worst? You have to be as careful with psychological symptoms. Consulting a psychologist for initial advice could help you understand how to best manage your difficulty.*

•AVOID DIY →It often happens that the most reckless take drugs without any medical supervision, perhaps recovering the tablets of another family member or the prescribed droplets some time ago for a similar situation. Psychodrugs have specific effects on our organism and taking them without first consulting a doctor means putting your health at risk. The same goes for natural remedies for anxiety. Consulting an experienced professional is essential to effectively resolve the situation.

•*RELAXATION* →*There are many ways to discharge anxiety and negative energies. Exercise, take a walk in the countryside or in the high mountains. If you have a dog carve out time to play with him. Animals have extraordinary empathic power and improve our mood with their presence. It is no coincidence that they are widely used in pet therapy.*

•*PAMPER YOURSELF* →*At the end of the day, fill the bathtub with essential oils and enjoy the silence and warm water. Turn off tablets, mobile phones and computers, pull out colored pencils and relax by coloring the mandalas. This manual and expressive technique, which we abandoned growing up, will make us take a dip of memories in the past as well as favor our concentration, drive away toxic and negative thoughts.*

•*EXPRESSING ONESELF*→*Anxiety often arises from the conflict between what we would like to be and what we find ourselves doing, forced by social norms, family expectations and commitments. Find yourself, give vent to your nature, follow your instincts and find the courage to say no. We can say no to the boss, to my envious colleague, to the mother-in-law who criticises us, to the partner who ignores us. You start building stakes to defend yourself and you see that things are definitely going to get better.*

•*DO WITHOUT THINKING NOW*→*Seizing the moment is the best way to avoid postponing actions and decisions, a very common trend in case of depression, but one that risks moving us even further away from the flow of life. In order to overcome sadness, it is essential to take back the reins of one's destiny. It doesn't matter if the mood and intentions aren't the best; to see a change, instead of sitting down, get up and act.*

•REDISCOVER MANUAL SKILLS →Manual work helps to face difficult situations from a new point of view, increases self-awareness and allows you to observe the concrete product of your actions, creating a situation of natural well-being. Whether it's cooking, painting, creating, diying, it's important to focus on the gestures that are made and only on those. This empties the mind of conditioning and worries, thus favoring the natural production of substances that promote joy and happiness.

•LOOK AT REALITY AS IT IS →Overcoming depression is a challenge to be won firsthand. That's why, every time you face an adverse event, don't blame fate or bad luck, but start wondering what you've put in place. Only in this way can you really modify harmful conduct and habits that are an obstacle to the achievement of any goal, such as renunciation, mistrust, destructive sarcasm....

•*IMMERSE YOURSELF IN NATURE* →*Being in contact with nature, caring for a plant or an animal helps to overcome the closure towards the world and what surrounds you, allows you to shift the obsessive attention focused only on you towards something totally different, which has nothing to do with thoughts and reasoning. Dealing with plants and animals makes you feel important, useful: the feeling of being indispensable allows you to put aside depression and stretcher, pushing you to regain interest and energy.*

•*TRAIN AT DETACHMENT* →*The more you are bound and dependent on something, be it goods, people or beliefs, the more you find yourself trapped in a form of possession that binds well-being and personal identity to their presence. Happiness, in these cases, always depends on circumstances independent of your will. On the contrary, with the right detachment you return to give value to your freedom and the authenticity that characterizes you deeply.*

•STOP THE LAMENTS →Crying on yourself is the best way to dissipate important energies that could be used constructively. Then, no one likes the laments and in times of greatest distress you risk finding yourself even more alone, helping to define a negative and losing image of you. In the long run, the risk is to incur the infamous self-chasing prophecies.

•YES TO HEALTHY SELFISHNESS →Learn to be demanding first of all with yourself. Do not listen to those who offer you advice that you do not feel you approve of: trust only your instincts and satisfy your needs, those that flow from within and define who you are, without falling victim to a false moral packaged from the outside. You will gain in confidence and personality.

•*USE IMAGINATION→Focus your mind exclusively on pleasant images and events. Can you remember the last time you felt happy, capable and satisfied? All you have to do is re-taste those same sensations: the eyes that shone, the sense of power, a wave of energy. Several times a day, he comes back with his mind to those moments; little by little, you will feel less intolerable sadness and depression.*

•*FREE YOUR MIND WITH SPORT→Physical activity is an excellent outlet valve, through which it is possible to counteract anxiety, stress and depression. Sport also promotes the production of brain substances (endorphins, dopamine, serotonin and norepinephrine) that enhance mood tone, improve the general condition of well-being and fight black humor.*

•*HOLD BACK JUDGMENT* →*Thinking that your value is solely related to the results obtained and the possibility of having carried out your projects involves excessive identification with objectives and reasoning often present only in the superficial mind. Failure of a project does not mean and does not necessarily imply your failure as an individual.*

•*STOP RATIONALITY* →*When you tend to manage and organize life using only your head, trying to control and rationalize everything, you just risk making yourself more fragile and opening the door to disequieting and depression. Every now and then, do something carefree and with no apparent purpose and let some healthy spontaneity find space in your day: to combat depression reason is not necessary, while it is of great help to lose every now and then that obsessive control that in the long run only gives suffering.*

THE IMPORTANCE OF PSYCHOLOGICAL SUPPORT

The goal of treatment is to reduce the number of heart attacks and their intensity. Psychological interventions are often used for the treatment of panic disorder.

PET THERAPY

When we talk about pet therapy we mean all those activities carried out in contact with service animals (dogs and cats for the most part) to solve and treat disorders such as stress and anxiety. Although abroad it is not known by this term, pet therapy in Italy has been very successful, so much so that it was officially recognized in 2002 by the Ministry of Health. What is pet therapy?

Pet therapy is more than just an alternative medicine and one of the most recommended pathways for the elderly, children and young people with autism or other forms of mental and physical disability. The passage of valuable time in contact with pets such as dogs and cats has shown that most psycho-social discomforts and the bio-physical sphere have been improved in patients. Simply walking a dog to the park, stroking a cat while reading a book or listening to music, taking care of them by brushing them or feeding them causes the patient to identify as a friend (social sphere) but also as the animal's manager, making sure that in this way he learns to be autonomous and more confident in daily actions. Therefore pet therapy is considered not only for therapeutic purposes but also as an educational and gaming moment. Interactions between patient and pet stimulate emotions in them and cause new interests and ways of communicating to arise. Another piece that serves for the correct usability and effectiveness of pet therapy is the presence of an experienced and educated staff, able to accompany the patient in his path, know the animal and know how to manage with safety and tranquility the whole period of therapy, play and learning.

The perfect animals for pet therapy

There is no right or wrong animal for this therapy, although often and willingly the most present are dogs, cats, horses, donkeys and rabbits. What is needed, whatever animal is chosen is that it is certified by a veterinarian experienced in pet therapy who will assess whether the animal in question has all the health and behavioral requirements to play this important role. It is also essential that in addition to the patient and the animal there is a third figure, namely the conductor, the one who trains and educates the pet for pet therapy. Their relationship and understanding must be very strong so that there are good final results and the conductor will be present alongside his animal throughout the journey.

Dog therapy with Labradors

The dog, however, remains the most present pet during pet therapy sessions, precisely for this reason a name of its own, dog therapy, has been dedicated. Not all breeds are suitable, among the most common and used in this important "work" are labradors, both adults but also labrador puppies, especially indicated for patients who have motor difficulties that prevent them from large movements and movements. Labrador dogs are very suitable for this type of therapy as they are faithful and lively animals, in them there is no psychological mechanism behind the bond with the patient but purely the desire to play and give affection. They are also able to understand the language of the human body and perceive the emotional state that we transmit with hormonal secretions, such as anxiety, stress, fear and sadness. And it is thanks to this ability that dogs are suitable for therapy as they are able to respond to these perceptions with play, liveliness, pampering and affection. Dogs, but like all animals, do not judge who they face and this favors that on the other side there is no longer the fear of saying or doing what you feel and feels, that is why they favor new ways of communicating, which often come to be missed in patients such as the elderly or autistic children. It has long been stressed that children suffering from stress interacting with therapy dogs benefit from improved mood and reduced anxiety. Researchers at Yale University reported that unspin structured interactions with a therapy dog stimulated children's positive emotions as a result of a stressful moderator compared to children who received a soothing object (a soft blanket) or those who simply waited a short time without intervention. Even children who interacted with a dog had less distress than those waiting. The Good Dog Foundation helped establish study protocols that clarified the effects of pet therapy with dogs, prioritizing both human and human safety and well-being. The organization also provided certified therapy teams to participate in the study. Human dog therapy teams are widely available in healthcare and school throughout the United States. The study states that "interactions with animals represent a promising way to reduce the weight of *childhood mental illness on a large scale" and, while more research is needed, their presence is increasingly supported by a growing scientific body on the effectiveness of the animals in the assisted interactions. The Institute for Research on Human-Animal Ties (HABRI) funded the study to better understand the emotional and physiological effects on children caused by canine members of cynophile teams. Studies have previously assessed the effects of dogs and handlers together, while this study examined the impact a dog could have. The Yale team has highlighted two important results: dogs alone can improve children's mood and ability to cope with anxiety and can do so as a therapeutic intervention for stress recovery. The study included pre-adolescent children (ages 10-13) because they are particularly susceptible to treatment obstacles such as perceived stigma, discomfort that speaks of mental health problems, and who want to cope independently, plus therapy dogs are already widely used for children this age group. The children were randomized into three groups: those who played with a dog, those placed in a tactile stimulation control group with a soft blanket, and those in a waiting control group. Among the dogs (four males, four females) who contributed to the data collection, all were certified as therapy dogs by the Good Dog Foundation or another therapy dog organization (e.g., Pet Partners). Prior to exposure to children, all dogs were familiar with laboratory settings and screened for the adequacy of study procedures. To protect the safety and well-being of human and canine participants during the 15-minute interventions, an experimenter oversaw all interactions from the corner of the room. The dogs' handlers themselves also observed from behind a two-way mirror. The physiological stress of children was tested through salivary cortisol levels throughout the duration of the study. Participants in the three study arms did not differ in terms of age, race/ethnicity, gender, dog experience, or other measures that explore children's feelings and behavior toward pets. Following exposure to stressful activity, children interacting with a dog showed significantly higher levels of positive effects than participants who received tactile* stimulation without any interaction (p = 0.007) or expected (an average difference of 1.92 points (p = 0.025). In addition, children playing with a dog had significantly lower anxiety scores than participants in the waiting condition (an average difference of 3.63 points; p = 0.003) No statistical difference was found between those in the tactile stimulation control condition (p = 0.065) and those interacting with dogs. Molly K. Crossman, lead author of the study at Yale University's Department of Psychology, commented, "The interesting thing is that the study brings us closer to the question of whether there is anything special about dogs, in terms of their ability to help children recover from stress. They are doing something better than another common coping strategy – tactile stimulation from a calming object – and that deserves further research so that effective and efficient interventions can be built. We are grateful to The Good Dog Foundation for their role in helping establish dog selection and care protocols and connecting with a number of outstanding dog teams, which have been essential to the success of the project.

" Good Dog Foundation board director Heidi Greene and her dog, Deuce, who participated in the Yale study, have worked together as a certified therapy team for over a decade. She explains and thanks for the collaboration: "We mostly volunteer in psychiatric facilities and with children in reading programs. We saw how a short visit and Deuce's pampering can bring the necessary comfort. But, working with yale's study group to help codify how dogs help humans heal was electrifying, a particular privilege. As an organization, The Good Dog Foundation is committed to initiating and participating in research with esteemed academic partners such as Yale. It is part of our mission to broaden the evidence base and our understanding of human-animal interaction."

After all, you know, drugs aren't everything...

Epilogue

And here we are, at the end of our journey of knowledge of the horrible and difficult world that live all those who, even if in a small part, are affected by one or even all three at the same time the invisible monsters. Unfortunately, even today in 2021 there are people who are not able to understand or at least have the sensitivity not to bully those who have the misfortune to meet monsters often inducing them to suicide. I hope that in my small way, I can give strength to those like me who fight every day against these beasts and a little teachings and moral values to the ignorant and poor in mind who judge us. Remember that those who fight for this, are special people, unique, rare and with a great beautiful and pure soul; do not get discouraged and do not demur, nature has something extremely wonderful waiting for you.

Irene.